THE
LANAHAN
CASES
IN
LEADERSHIP,
ETHICS &
DECISION-MAKING

THE
LANAHAN
CASES
IN
LEADERSHIP,
ETHICS &
DECISION-MAKING

edited by
Douglas M. Brattebo
Eloise F. Malone
UNITED STATES NAVAL ACADEMY

with the assistance of
Ann G. Serow
KINGSWOOD-OXFORD SCHOOL

LANAHAN PUBLISHERS, INC. *Baltimore*

The text of this book was composed in Bembo
with display type set in
Garamond and Bernhard Modern Roman.
Composition by Bytheway Publishing Services
Manufacturing by Victor Graphics, Inc.

ISBN 1-930398-01-8

LANAHAN PUBLISHERS, INC.
324 Hawthorne Road, Baltimore, MD 21210
1-866-345-1949 (toll free)

3 4 5 6 7 8 9 0

CONTENTS

PREFACE

THIS BOOK HAS TAKEN shape over a period of years as a volume to be read by all fourth class (freshman) midshipmen at the U.S. Naval Academy as part of their introductory course on American Government. It is a collection of writings about leadership in the American political system, both its constitutional and ethical foundations and its practice by individuals in trying settings. The selection of these essays has been determined in large part by the reactions of midshipmen over more than a decade, as these future Naval Officers have indicated that certain pieces have profoundly affected their thinking about their government and their leaders. It thus is destined to remain a work in progress, as new history is made and as the midshipmen of the future call to the attention of their instructors certain tracts that have made a difference. That is as it should be, for the Naval Academy exists to produce naval officers capable of exercising leadership within our constitutional system, and fulfilling that mission requires constant reappraisal. So, too, does the hard work of kindling within undergraduates everywhere the spark necessary to think with precision and passion about their political heritage and the leadership challenges of today and tomorrow. We are hopeful that this book will be a useful aid in that undertaking on campuses of all kinds.

Part One of the book comprises four essays concerned with the philosophical and institutional foundations of leadership in the American system. E. M. Halliday (*Nature's God and the Founding Fathers*) describes Thomas Jefferson and James Madison's views on the relationship between church and state, providing a detailed account of their efforts to craft the First Amendment. Halliday reminds us how unconventional and far-sighted these two Enlightenment thinkers were in their views about religious freedom and democracy. Kenneth R. Bowling (*'A Tub to the Whale': The Adoption of the Bill of Rights*) demonstrates that there was nothing inevitable about the entire Bill of Rights, which came about as a grand political bargain between the federalists and anti-federalists to clinch the ratification of the new Constitution. The Framers, Bowling points out, were pragmatists who understood that compromise is at the heart of democracy, and that the perfect cannot be the enemy of the good. Thurgood Marshall (*Reflections on the Bicentennial of the United States Constitution*) argues that Americans embrace too uncritically the American cultural mythology that portrays the Constitution as a perfect document framed by a cadre of infallible, altruistic philosophers. The secret to the Constitution's success and longevity, he states, has been its ability to change in ways the Framers might neither have anticipated nor approved. Richard D. Brown (*Where Have All the Great Men Gone?*) compares the way presidential candidates were selected during the Republic's early period with the way they are chosen today, and identifies clear reasons why each system stresses certain characteristics in potential leaders. In a sense, Brown brings the discussion full circle. He suggests that, although we may take a harsh view of our contemporary leaders and romanticize the Framers' character and their feats of leadership, they still were a remarkable group of theorists and practitioners by any measure.

Part Two of the book consists of eight cases that emphasize the challenges faced by leaders in extraordinary settings. Some of these figures rose to the occasion, bracing themselves to their duty and succeeding in whole or in part, while others fell short of the applicable ethical and constitutional standards. The first three readings explore leadership dilemmas during the Republic's founding, early evolution, and great trial by civil war. James Thomas Flexner (*Washington: The Indispensable Man*) reminds us that no hyperbole is involved in labeling George Washington as the father of this country. In few other instances in the nation's history has the character of one leader made so decisive a difference. Washington could have been king or dictator by popular demand, but he instead made certain the Republic was birthed, establishing in the process the precedent of civilian control over the military. Paul C. Nagel (*John Adams: A Public Life, A Private Life*) examines the struggle of John Quincy Adams to exert direction over the course of the nation during his post-presidential years. For Adams, the most efficacious way to strike a blow for abolition was to make a stand for the procedural tenets of democracy, both in the House of Representatives and in Federal Court. Adams, tempestuous and abrasive in a decidedly un-Washingtonian fashion, exhibited great fidelity to his principles and influenced the debate over slavery at a crucial juncture. Stephen Oates (*With Malice Toward None: The Life of Abraham Lincoln*) charts the Herculean efforts of Abraham Lincoln to hold the tenuous center in American politics during the early phases of the Civil War. The President reached beyond his explicit constitutional authority to prosecute the war and save the Constitution, yet he was chastened by the exercise of power and sought to retain some semblance of normality in his daily life. For Lincoln during the Republic's greatest tribulation, as with Washington during its making moment, character was destiny.

The next three readings of Part Two concentrate on the dilemmas that leaders in the twentieth century have confronted during war with foreign nations. Chief Justice William H. Rehnquist (*When the Laws Were Silent*) recounts the manner in which President Franklin Roosevelt ordered the internment of all Japanese-Americans during the Second World War. Congress supported his decision, and the Supreme Court upheld it. Rehnquist's study is a reminder of the way that the exigencies of war can threaten the equal protection of a certain group of citizens if leaders and public opinion permit it. Doris Kearns Goodwin (*No Ordinary Time*) examines the effects of wartime on the rights and lives of a condemned minority abroad. Goodwin describes the extraordinary political partnership of Franklin and Eleanor Roosevelt, noting the frequent tension between Eleanor's progressive politics and Franklin's more pragmatic political concerns as he worked to steer the Allies toward victory. Eleanor urged the President to take the administrative and military steps necessary to disrupt the slaughter of the European Jews, but Franklin could not bring himself to spend the required political capital and divert the war materiel necessary to champion their cause fully. David McCullough (*Truman*) tells of the titanic struggle between President Harry Truman and General Douglas MacArthur over who would make policy in the Korean War. Truman fired the legendary General after MacArthur repeatedly crossed the line of insubordination, even though the President knew he would face a firestorm of criticism in the short run. The idea of civilian control over the military had to be unpheld at a crucial moment, Truman believed, and history has vindicated his principled stand.

The last two readings of Part Two focus on two of the most troubling constitutional crises of the twentieth century. Walter Karp and Vance Bourjaily (*The Triumph of Watergate*) sketch the flow of events in Watergate, explaining how the reporting of a seemingly run-of-the-mill burglary ultimately revealed a spate of crimes of the most serious nature by President Richard Nixon. Nixon's resignation, the authors remind us, was not only a national trauma but also a vindication of Alexander Hamilton's contention that the Unites States is a country of laws, not merely of people. Finally, Lawrence E. Walsh (*Firewall*) lays out the myriad facts of the Iran-Contra Scandal, emphasizing the perils of a cabal within government whose members believed that they had the right and duty to substitute their own policy judgments for the rule of law. President Ronald Reagan knowingly broke both his own policy pronouncements and also the laws of the land, and he did so with the enthusiastic help of his high-ranking national security officials and staffers. It is fitting that this volume should conclude with Iran-Contra, for its failure to trigger the same public anger and depth of understanding as Watergate is a reminder that the future of republican government always hangs in the balance.

Finally, special thanks go out to two people for their help in creating this volume: First, Naval Academy graduate, Rhodes Scholar, and submariner Lieutenant Sean M. Fahey, currently an instructor in the Naval Academy's department of political science, was most helpful in evaluating the readings that made it (and those that didn't) into this reader. He also made valuable suggestions about how the readings would complement one another.

Second, Dr. Ann G. Serow of Kingswood-Oxford School provided crucial counsel in helping this book take shape. She suggested readings as candidates for inclusion, and several of them have become a part of this volume. Her attention to detail has resulted in articles with a more precise editorial thrust, and she has encouraged consistency in the structure and pedagogy of the work.

Douglas M. Brattebo
Eloise F. Malone
Annapolis, Maryland
May 2001

THE
LANAHAN
CASES
IN
LEADERSHIP,
ETHICS &
DECISION-MAKING

PART ONE

FOUNDATIONS

1 Nature's God and the Founding Fathers

E. M. HALLIDAY

The final decision on how to word the freedom of religion clause of the First Amendment was the result of a long series of discussions among the Founders of the nation: "Congress shall make no law respecting an establishment of religion or prohibiting the free exercise thereof . . . " In this article, E. M. Halliday explains that there were several precursors to this wording, for there was religious diversity among the Founders. However, there was also among them a belief in a moral order in large part derived from the ideas of the European Enlightenment. High among these ideas was freedom of conscience. Examine this idea as you see how the nation's early leaders struggled and ultimately avoided the dangers of establishing a national religion and of prohibiting any individual's or group's practice of belief.

FROM HIS PULPIT in Christ Episcopal Church in Philadelphia, Dr. James Abercrombie looked out at a congregation that included the first President of the United States. He had good reason to feel some nervousness on this particular Sunday morning, for he was about to perform an act of ecclesiastical daring. He was about to scold George Washington, in public, for his religious behavior.

Dr. Abercrombie mentioned no names as he pitched into a sermon on the grave responsibility of "those in elevated stations" to set good examples for lesser folk, but only the children in his pews that day could have missed the point. He focused on the celebration of the Lord's Supper; and everyone knew that President Washington habitually joined those who walked out of church, on communion Sundays, just before the sacrament was to be administered. The rector's target was embarrassingly clear.

No doubt Dr. Abercrombie hoped to achieve the pious triumph of persuading the President to take holy communion at his altar. But, although his message had not passed the presidential ears unheeded, the outcome was disconcerting. Washington never again left the church just before the Lord's Supper — from that time forward he did not come at all on communion Sundays.

The minister swallowed his disappointment as best he could. Writing, years later, to someone who had inquired about Washington's religion, he said that according to one of the President's acquaintances — he could not remember precisely whom — the great man preferred to stay away rather than become a communicant because, "were he to become one then, it would be imputed to an ostentatious display of religious zeal." This was a relatively consoling explanation, but there are signs that it failed to convince Dr. Abercrombie himself. "That Washington was a professing Christian," he added to his correspondent, "is evident from his regular attendance in our church, but sir, I cannot consider any man as a real Christian who uniformly disregards an ordinance so solemnly enjoined by the divine Author of our holy religion. . . ."

What were Washington's reasons for refusing to partake in the Lord's Supper? Exact answers are lost to history, concealed behind the reticence he steadily maintained where his private beliefs were concerned. In terms of reasonable inference, however, it is possible to offer an explanation. He had long been exposed to the ideas of the European Enlightenment, and his behavior suggests that his religious views were considerably shaped thereby. It was an intellectual atmosphere not favorable to symbolic rites, among other things. In his exposure to it, Washington was of course far from unique among the Founding Fathers of the American republic. Inevitably, all of his educated contemporaries were to some extent children of the Age of Reason (as Tom Paine called it); and among them several of the acknowledged political leaders were certainly its eminent sons.

Still, there was no great uniformity of opinion among the Founding Fathers on specific religious or philosophical questions. Whether one considers the signers of the Declaration of Independence or the delegates to the Constitutional Convention of 1787, or both, it is easy to find a diversity of sects and creeds. But the broad spectrum of denominations is itself a reminder that a prime characteristic of the Enlightenment was respect for dissenting opinions. The famous remark attributed to Voltaire, "I may disagree with what you say, but I will defend to the death your right to say it," catches the spirit of the era. While full freedom of belief was not legally protected in any of the colonies at the start of the Revolution, and most of them had an established church supported by the government, minority groups and nonconforming individuals were in fact granted considerable leeway. Catholics were strong in Maryland; Quakers, in Pennsylvania. In New England, the evolution of Congregational doctrine had moved toward freedom of conscience for more than a century, so that there was a kind of paradox in the legal establishment of a church so nearly democratic in its organization. The supremacy of the Anglicans in the South, moreover, was weakened by the fact that theirs was the official church of England in a period when independence from the mother country was about to become the paramount fact of current history. For, whatever their doctrinal differences in religion, all of the Founding Fathers were political revolutionaries, determined to enact a new formulation of the idea of government by consent of the governed.

Even Washington's most ardent admirers have never claimed that he was, philosophically, a deep thinker. Thomas Jefferson, by contrast, was as philosophically inclined, and gifted with as keen an analytical mind, as any American of his time. His interest in religion and its proper relationship to government was intense, and it persisted throughout his long life. During his second term as President (1805–1809) he sought relief from the tremendous pressures of his office by composing, for his own satisfaction, a version of the New Testament which he called "The Life and Morals of Jesus of Nazareth." It would have interested Washington, for among many other significant omissions it pointedly left out the story of the Last Supper. This was as good a clue as any to Jefferson's idea in undertaking the work, which was, in his own sharp language, to rescue from "the speculations of crazy theologists" the moral teachings of Jesus, "abstracting what is really his from the rubbish in which it is buried."

In his own terms, Jefferson claimed to be a Christian—but he assuredly was not one according to Dr. Abercrombie's standards, or for that matter according to the doctrine of any organized Christian church, unless it was the fledgling Unitarian. He rejected, he wrote, "the immaculate conception of Jesus, his deification, the creation of the world by him, his miraculous powers, his resurrection and visible ascension, his corporeal presence in the Eucharist, the Trinity, original sin, atonement, regeneration, election, orders of Hierarchy, etc." He thought of Christ as a great reformer, author of "a system of the most sublime morality which has ever fallen from the lips of man"—but human rather than divine. To be a Christian, for Jefferson, was simply to follow the system of ethics taught by Christ, uncontaminated by what he considered the additions, adulterations, and distortions of those who came after. And Jefferson thought he had an easy touchstone for distinguishing Jesus' original teachings from the dross. All that was needed was the "free exercise of reason": with that, the genuine precepts of the Master would never be found to disagree.

To orthodox clergymen and theologians this was heresy; it was, many of them angrily charged, a mere disguise for atheism. As a prominent political figure, Jefferson often suffered from his refusal to accept traditional Christianity, even though he tried to keep his religious views largely to himself. His skepticism toward anything alleged to be supernatural was misunderstood, and his high regard for Christian ethics was usually ignored. Shocking stories circulated long before he became a presidential candidate, and their currency grew with his fame. John Trumbull, the great painter of the Revolution, told one about a dinner party at Jefferson's home in 1793, when the future President sat "smiling and nodding approbation" while Congressman William Giles of Virginia — a fellow skeptic — "proceeded so far . . . as to ridicule the character, conduct and doctrines of the divine founder of our religion." This was unquestionably an exaggeration, but it suggests Jefferson's reputation at the time. When he was presidential runner-up in 1796, a minister in Connecticut took note of the event in a prayer before his congregation: "O Lord! wilt Thou bestow upon the Vice President a double portion of Thy grace, for *Thou knowest he needs it.*" In the campaign of 1800 Jefferson's "infidelity" was an easy target for Federalist orators and pamphleteers.

Yet there is little doubt that Jefferson held a profound belief in a Supreme Being. In a fashion typical of eighteenth-century intellectuals, he held it not on implicit faith, but as a reasoned conclusion based on evidence and deduction. "I hold (without appeal to revelation)," he once wrote to John Adams, "that when we take a view of the universe, in its parts, general or particular, it is impossible for the human mind not to perceive and feel a conviction of design, consummate skill, and indefinite power in every atom of its composition." Newton and his contemporaries in the seventeenth century had magnificently demonstrated that man lived in a universe of precise mathematical law and order; it seemed scientifically evident to most thinkers in the following era that such a cosmic design could come only from the hand of a divine Creator.

It was a long way from the theology of traditional Christianity — this idea of an invisible but demonstrable God whose existence was proved only by His handiwork — for "He" was now a nearly impersonal power, responsible for the origin and laws of the universe, but not interfering in its operation once the myriad wheels of the great machine had been set in motion. This was "Nature's God," as Jefferson phrased it in the Declaration of Independence; and to him and many others the religion appropriate to Nature's God must be natural, not supernatural, in its foundations. Deism, or "natural religion," expressed their theological creed, not a Christianity based on revelation, mystery, and miracle.

Some men—notably a prominent group in France including Diderot, d'Alembert, Condorcet, and the Baron d'Holbach—went further, postulating an automatic universe, operating by inexorable natural laws, but utterly devoid of God or God's purpose. Jefferson was inclined to resist this surge toward atheism, yet it is only justice to the true character of his mind to emphasize that his attitude was far from fanatical. He was never an absolutist, even on the question of God's existence. His creed of intellectual freedom was much too firm for that, and at worst he saw no alarming threat in atheism. Before he went to France to be United States minister from 1784 to 1789, he had already considered the effects of full disbelief. "It does me no injury for my neighbor to say there are twenty Gods, or no God," he observed in his *Notes on Virginia* (1782). "It neither picks my pocket nor breaks my leg." And writing to his young nephew, Peter Carr, from Paris in 1787, he urged him to make reason his guide: " . . . call to her tribunal every fact, every opinion. Question with boldness even the existence of a God; because, if there be one, he must more approve of the homage of reason, than that of blindfolded fear."

Jefferson's vital disposition toward freedom of thought was strengthened by his five years in France. Not only was he there a first-hand observer of the moral and material degradation resulting, as he saw it, from the combination of religious persecution and tyrannical government. In that cosmopolitan air he also made familiar contact with many of the most brilliant figures of the age. The political, philosophical, and religious ideas of the Enlightenment now reached him not just in books, but in absorbing conversations across his own dinner table. Voltaire had written that atheists, deplorable as they might be, would still make better neighbors than religious fanatics. Jefferson came to know some of the leading French atheists as friends and acquaintances, and he found them anything but monsters. "Diderot, D'Alembert, D'Holbach, Condorcet," he wrote to a friend years later, "are known to have been among the most virtuous of men. Their virtue, then, must have had some other foundation than the love of God."

This crucial question of the basis of human morality, bearing as it does on the relation between religion and government, intrigued Jefferson all his life. He early formed an opinion consistent with the natural religion of the Enlightenment, and from it he never swerved throughout the remainder of his eighty-three years. Its essence was natural morality. "Man was destined for society," he wrote to his nephew in 1787. " . . . He was endowed with a sense of right and wrong, merely relative to this. This sense is as much a part of his nature, as the sense of hearing, seeing, feeling; it is the true foundation of morality. . . . The moral sense, or conscience, is as much a part of man as his leg or arm." And while Jefferson firmly believed that this moral sense was the gift of a divine Creator, he was equally certain that acknowledgment of its source was not necessary to its function. If young Peter Carr, having fully considered the evidence, were to become an atheist, still, Jefferson assured him, "you will find incitements to virtue in the comfort and pleasantness you feel in its exercise, and the love of others which it will procure you."

Jefferson's theory of natural morality was for him the cornerstone of the democratic faith which he did so much during his lifetime to make a living reality. The church doctrine of original sin was anathema to him. Human nature could be trusted: all normal men were endowed by their Creator not only with unalienable rights, but with unalienable instincts, including a natural moral sense. Except under bad social conditions— ignorance, poor education, poverty—the mass of men, he felt, would surely gravitate toward what was right on fundamental issues, if only they were allowed complete freedom of conscience. The principle of majority rule—a sacred principle to Jefferson—depended on the premise of a well-informed public, each member of which could choose among moral or political alternatives with absolute freedom from mental coercion.

This is the key to Jefferson's lifelong insistence on complete separation of church and state. While it was a matter of democratic principle with him to champion full freedom of voluntary association, so that any number of divergent sects could thrive without government interference, he had no sympathy for their dogmatic approach to questions of moral truth. An organized church, he thought, was unlikely to leave men's minds completely free. . . .

Jefferson had the good fortune to live long and to compose his own epitaph after much deliberation. It was a modest statement for a man who had been among the foremost in establishing the American nation. He wished his tombstone to cite him in three capacities only: "Author of the Declaration of American Independence; of the Statute of Virginia for Religious Freedom; and Father of the University of Virginia." The order was chronological, but in a most important sense the three accomplishments were one and indivisible. The Declaration of Independence envisaged a free society ruled by consent of the governed. But informed decision and consent could be based only on good public education; and good education, in turn, could be based only on complete freedom of the mind. In the history of the new republic the first fundamental challenge to freedom of the mind came in the area of religion.

It is a curious fact of American history that the man who was inseparably associated with Jefferson in his fight for religious freedom, and who was to become his closest friend for nearly half a century, grew up only thirty-odd miles from Monticello, yet never met him until late in 1776. James Madison of Montpelier, in Port Conway, Virginia, came to the capitol at Williamsburg in May of that year, an elected delegate to the state convention. By that time, Jefferson was off to his appointment with fame in Philadelphia, and so the two did not meet until the following autumn — and even then their contact was slight. But in the meantime something had happened at Williamsburg to form a bond between them no less strong for its resting temporarily unperceived.

The government of Virginia was in process of being overhauled in the spring of 1776, and although young Madison, a relatively unknown delegate, did not have a great deal to do with the new state constitution, he was a member of a committee appointed to draw up a bill of rights. The great George Mason of Gunston Hall was chief author of the articles in this bill, which was to become the prototype for similar manifestoes in other states as well as, eventually, for the Bill of Rights of the United States Constitution.

It must have cheered Jefferson to see that prominent among the Virginia articles was one on religious freedom. Madison was instrumental in giving that article its final and significant form when the committee proposal went before the Virginia convention on June 12, 1776. Only five years out of college at Princeton, he was already an accomplished student of constitutional law, a man cast very much in Jefferson's mold. As he saw it, Mason's expression of the principle of religious freedom was deficient in two respects: it allowed for continuation of a state-supported church, and it spoke of "toleration in the exercise of religion" rather than absolute freedom of conscience. Recognizing that it was not quite time to push for disestablishment in Virginia, Madison let that go, but proposed a rewording that would move forward from the idea of mere toleration (which implied the right of the state either to grant or withhold religious freedom) to that of freedom of conscience as an unalienable natural right. The convention was not willing to go quite that far, but, in its permanent form, the article pronounced that "all men are equally entitled to the free exercise of religion, according to the dictates of conscience." It was a quiet yet important triumph in the struggle for complete liberty of thought in America. . . .

. . . [T]he Bill for Religious Freedom must have exerted a strong attractive force between Jefferson and Madison. They were now often in close consultation, Jefferson as newly elected governor, Madison as a member of his executive council; their personal friendship was also growing fast. Although Madison had been, from his college days, more skeptical and less orthodox than he has been painted by many biographers, his commitment to absolute freedom of thought as the undergirding of a free society was henceforth more intense. By the time Jefferson left for France, Madison was well prepared to carry on their campaign not only in Virginia, but in the first Congress, to which he would go as a representative in 1789.

In Virginia, Madison's skill finally brought victory for Jefferson's disestablishment bill, but not without a tough running battle against an opposition headed by the redoubtable Patrick Henry. . . .

Meanwhile, Madison was by no means impotent on the other side of the issue. He anonymously wrote his now famous "Memorial and Remonstrance Against Religious Assessments" (1785), which was circulated wide and far in Virginia as a petition to which thousands signed their names in protest against the renewed prospect of religious establishment. As copy after copy of the petition, crowded with signatures, streamed into the Virginia Assembly, it became very clear that the majority of the people were in no mood to forsake the religious freedom they had been promised by the 1776 Declaration of Rights. The surprised proponents of the assessment bill never even bothered to bring it to a vote.

Madison's "Remonstrance" was a piece of shrewd political propaganda. It struck a chord more in harmony with the orthodox Christianity of those to whom it was addressed than his private views might have sustained, yet it echoed the rationalist strain of his religious discussions with Jefferson.

In fifteen paragraphs, many of them harking back to the popular article on religion in the 1776 Declaration of Rights, he argued against government support of the church. Every man's religion, he wrote,

> must be left to the conviction and conscience of every man; and it is the right of every man to exercise it as these may dictate. This right is in its nature an unalienable right . . . because the opinions of men, depending only on the evidence contemplated by their own minds, cannot follow the dictates of other men. . . . We maintain therefore that in matters of Religion, no man's right is abridged by the institution of Civil Society, and that Religion is wholly exempt from its cognizance. . . . Who does not see that the same authority which can establish Christianity, in exclusion of all other Religions, may establish with the same ease any particular sect of Christians, in exclusion of all other Sects? . . . Whilst we assert for ourselves a freedom to embrace, to

profess, and to observe the Religion which we believe to be of divine origin, we cannot deny an equal freedom to those whose minds have not yet yielded to the evidence which has convinced us. . . .

It is noteworthy, since it bears on the meaning of the First Amendment to the Constitution, that to Madison and the thousands of Virginians who signed his petition, "establishment of religion" meant any government sponsorship of any or all religions, and not just the European pattern of an exclusive, official state church. (The "Remonstrance" refers repeatedly to Henry's general assessment bill as "the proposed establishment.") They wanted a solid "wall of separation between church and state," to use a phrase Jefferson invented later. Acting on the theory that a good time to dispatch an enemy was when he was on the run, Madison and his friends in the legislature now took Jefferson's Bill for Religious Liberty off the shelf where it had seasoned since 1779, and this time saw it voted in by a substantial majority. In principle it was a twin to Madison's "Remonstrance," but even more trenchant in its rhetoric and forthright in its defense of absolute freedom of thought and expressions — a forerunner, as well as, in a sense, an interpretation of the First Amendment to the Constitution. . . .

The example of Virginia — by far the largest of the thirteen states in population, and home of a cluster of distinguished men headed by the revered Washington — could hardly be ignored in the rest of America. The winds of revolution already had blown away much restrictive custom and legislation by 1786. Most of the other states had recently passed bills of rights honoring religious freedom, even though, with the exception of Rhode Island, New Jersey, and New York, they still had church establishment in at least the multiple form, embracing several sects. It was to be a number of years before any of them matched Virginia, yet it was natural that her action greatly strengthened the general current toward increased freedom of thought and an accompanying separation of church and state.

But it was to be almost by accident that the question of religious freedom first arose at the national level. The Constitutional Convention, gathering at Philadelphia in the spring of 1787, ignored it for many weeks — not because it was felt to be unimportant, but because it was considered the business of the states rather than of the central government. But as a hot August steamed into a hot September, it became obvious that the federal machinery designed by men like Madison, Alexander Hamilton, and Roger Sherman was far more powerful than the old Articles of Confederation. What about the rights of the people under such a government? They ought to be, asserted George Mason, "the pole star of political conduct." The state governments were, in 1787, the guardians of those rights; but the new Constitution greatly reduced the power of the states. With Mason at the center, a small nucleus of delegates began to agitate for specific guarantees, to be built into the Constitution itself. Charles Pinckney, of South Carolina, urged a ban on religious tests for federal officeholders, and the Convention — thinking, no doubt, of their own wide spread of religious opinion — quickly adopted it (Article VI).

Still, the movement for a full bill of rights, similar to those prevailing in a majority of the states, found little support. Mason was deeply disturbed, and announced that he would "sooner chop off his right hand than put it to the Constitution as it now stands." But Roger Sherman expressed the more general feeling when he said that "the State Declarations of Rights are not repealed by this Constitution; and being in force are sufficient." The tired delegates brought the Convention to a close on September 17, 1787, and the Constitution was submitted to the states without a bill of rights. Mason did not chop off his hand, but he did quit the Convention without signing.

As the contest over ratification swung back and forth in the various state legislatures during 1787–88, the federalists were forced to admit that a compromise was in order. From New England to Georgia there was intense pressure for a national bill of rights as a condition of ratification. Some federalists at first viewed this as nothing but camouflage for an attempt to frustrate ratification altogether. Alexander Hamilton was angry and contemptuous. It was the plan of the antifederalists, he declared, "to frighten the people with ideal bugbears, in order to mould them to their own purpose. The unceasing cry of these designing croakers is, 'My friends, your liberty is invaded!'" Washington, choosing somewhat milder language, was inclined to agree. . . .

Concern over individual liberty, of course, was by no means the exclusive property of antifederalists. Indeed, there were many on the other side (including Madison and Jefferson, both of whom must be counted as federalists at this early stage) who were as deeply devoted to liberty as anyone in the antifederalist ranks. Madison had been somewhat wary of a federal bill of rights for fear that specifying what the central government might not infringe would imply that it could suppress other rights, not enumerated. But reconsideration plus advice from Jefferson changed his mind; and numerous other important federalists finally conceded the expedience if not the need of such a bill. The upshot was that as the state conventions one by one ratified the Constitution, most of them did so with a strong recommendation for the addition of protective amendments. Madison found himself, in March of 1789, setting out from Virginia as a representative to the First Congress, pledged to introduce a large batch of amendments. Among them were, in substance, the ten that now make up the Bill of Rights.

With long congressional debates developing over such urgent matters as new revenue laws, and such intriguing ones as whether the Chief Executive should be called "His Highness" or just "the President," it was June before Madison was able to get any action on the proposed amendments. Even then there was some reluctance to discuss a national bill of rights in preference to questions of greater sectional interest, and he was obliged to lecture his House colleagues on what their constituents expected of them — particularly "those safeguards which they have been long accustomed to have interposed between them and the magistrate who exercises the sovereign power." He then presented his list of amendments and gave a long speech defending them. One prophetic point he made was in the form of a quotation from Jefferson saying that the federal courts would "consider themselves in a peculiar manner the guardians of those rights" stipulated in such amendments to the Constitution.

The congressional history of Madison's amendment on religion throws some interesting illumination on the question of just what it meant in its final form, when after much rewording it became part of the First Amendment. He first introduced it as, "The civil rights of none shall be abridged on account of religious belief or worship, nor shall any national religion be established, nor shall the full and equal rights of conscience be in any manner, or on any pretext, abridged." Against the background of the Jefferson-Madison view of religion in its relation to democratic government, the emphasis here is unmistakable. It goes straight to what they conceived to be the heart of the matter: absolute freedom of thought for the individual citizen without government pressure toward any system of belief whatever. It seems likely that, had Madison's original wording been adopted, official sanction for even the vague theism suggested by the motto first engraved on United States coins in 1864 ("In God We Trust"), or by the interpolation in 1954 of "under God" in the national oath of allegiance, would have been considered unconstitutional. . . .

Madison's original amendment on religion, however, was soon altered. It was referred to a committee of which he was vice-chairman, and evidently caused much discussion — although no exact committee records, unfortunately, were kept. On August 15, 1789, the House as a whole took up the question, considering it in a shorter and less explicit form ("No religion shall be established by law, nor shall the equal rights of conscience be infringed"). Although this wording was less forthright, some members were apprehensive of its effect: Peter Silvester, of New York, said that he "feared it might be thought to have a tendency to abolish religion altogether." The amendment was sent forward to the Senate as, "Congress shall make no law establishing religion, or to prevent the free exercise thereof, or to infringe the rights of conscience." There can be little question that the phrase "or to prevent the free exercise thereof" indicated a desire that the prohibition against establishment should not be interpreted as hostile to religion. . . .

. . . A joint committee, with Madison as chairman of the three House members and Oliver Ellsworth of Connecticut as his counterpart for the Senate . . . — again without leaving us minutes of their discussion — . . . came up with the wording that has become part of the First Amendment: "Congress shall make no law respecting an establishment of religion, or prohibiting the free exercise thereof." Madison could not have been pleased to see the key phrase about "the rights of conscience" abandoned — for him that clarified the basic intent of the amendment — but he was convinced that in its final form the first article of the Bill of Rights could be reasonably interpreted as prohibiting federal support of religious activities in any form.

That, as has been noted, was the way he and Jefferson interpreted it during their terms as President, and for the rest of their lives. At the same time, both of them realized that while they had led a successful campaign for separation of church and state as an essential footing in the structure of democracy, their theoretical reasons for doing so were grasped by relatively few of their countrymen. They knew their ideal was still remote: a society so free that its only ideological commitment would be to freedom of the mind. Much of the support they had been able to rally for a barrier between church and state had other sources. True, it sprang in part from a native intellectual current against absolutism which has never failed to flow in America despite counteracting currents of great force. But in part it came from the mutual and competitive mistrust of the various religious sects toward one another. Always pragmatic, Jefferson and Madison saw the value of this, despite their own rejection of revealed religion. Variety of belief was a useful insurance against tyranny.

The history of the First Amendment since 1791, when the last of the necessary eleven states ratified the federal Bill of Rights, has been one of fluctuating interpretation. This has been most notable during the last fifty years, during which, for the most part, the Supreme Court has found that the Fourteenth Amendment enjoins the guarantees of the First upon the states, for the protection of every citizen. There has been some confusion and inconsistency: schoolchildren swear allegiance to one nation "under God," yet cannot be led in official school prayers, however nonde-nominational. Over a period of years, however, the trend of Court deci-sions has been toward strict separation of church and state, in a manner that assuredly would please Jefferson and Madison if they were here to see it. Indeed, the Justices have shown a strong penchant for citing these champions of freedom in explaining and supporting recent Court decisions.

There is nothing sacred about the reasoning of any of our ancestors, on this or any other matter. But whether one agrees with Jefferson and Madison or not, with regard to how high and impassable the wall between church and state ought to stand in a free society, they deserve to be remembered and understood, as the two among the Founding Fathers who devoted more of their minds and lives to this great problem than anyone else. They were an intellectual *avant-garde* whose probing of the relationship between religion and democracy went beyond the more or less traditional attitudes of most Americans between 1776 and 1791. Yet they were the center of a high-pressure area in the climate of opinion of their time, and their conclusions were strongly reflected in the Constitu-tion as it finally was adopted.

Their thinking, moreover, can be fairly understood only as emerging from the matrix of the Enlightenment, of which — with such men as Benjamin Franklin, Thomas Paine, James Monroe, and even George Washington and John Adams — they were indubitably the intellectual offspring. The impact of "natural religion" on the genesis of democratic liberty, through their influence, has too often been ignored.

Writing to Dr. Benjamin Rush in 1800, shortly before he became President, Jefferson alleged certain clerical "schemes" to breach the religion clause of the First Amendment. He would oppose them with all his power, he said, "for I have sworn upon the altar of God eternal hostility against every form of tyranny over the mind of man." It was "Nature's God" that he was thinking of, and for that vow above all others the altar was not to be found, he believed, within the limits of any dogmatic creed.

Questions for Discussion

1.   Do you share Jefferson and Madison's belief that reason must be the most important determinant of a code of moral behavior? Are standards of morality constructed by human beings or merely discovered by them?

2.   Do absolute moral standards exist? If so, is it sensible to claim that any one religion is better at identifying them than another?

3.   Can shared moral beliefs coexist with religious pluralism? How does the First Amendment act to protect religion from government as well as to protect government from religion?

2 "A Tub to the Whale": The Adoption of the Bill of Rights

KENNETH R. BOWLING

It is easy to read the Constitution with its Bill of Rights, and think that it is and always has been set in stone. But during the writing, much was in dispute, especially whether there should be these civil-liberties amendments at all. The Founders of the nation were in pursuit of one goal, but they were not always of one mind. Only an amalgamation of leadership, ethics, and politics brought about these first ten amendments that have become the source of unforeseen and major judicial interpretation and litigation for over two hundred years.

THE ROLE OF THE FEDERAL Bill of Rights in American constitutional development has been monumental. This fact would have surprised most of the members of the first federal Congress, the body that reluctantly proposed to the states the amendments later called the Bill of Rights. The Federalist majority considered these amendments an unnecessary political expedient of little constitutional importance, and the time spent on them as wasted.

Although many Antifederalists had made many eloquent statements about the importance of a bill of rights during the ratification campaign, the Antifederal minority in Congress recognized that civil-liberty amendments could be advanced by Federalists as a means to divert attention away from the structural and states' rights amendments that they sought. Without the commitment of James Madison, who drafted the amendments and then, virtually begging, guided them, through the House of Representatives, there would have been no federal Bill of Rights in 1791. Although Madison believed bills of rights important for the protection of civil liberties, he led the fight for practical political reasons. But Madison was not a cynic, and historians who allude to his use of the phrase "nauseous project" to describe the process of getting amendments through the Congress quote the Virginian out of context. Madison was joking to a friend who had sent him a fable, entitled "The Wise Cooks and Foolish Guests," that told the story of how a delicious soup was made by eleven cooks (the ratifying states) was ruined when the guests insisted on various changes in the recipe.

In an anonymous attack on Madison, published while the Virginian led the floor fight for amendments, Noah Webster, although not a member of Congress, expressed the point of view of many of its Federalist members: "It seems to be agreed on all hands that paper declarations of rights are trifling things and no real security to liberty. In general they are a subject of ridicule." The nation regretted that "Congress should spend their time in throwing out an empty tub to catch people" and that "Madison's talents should be employed to bring forward amendments" which "can have little effect upon the merits of the constitution."

Webster's reference to the empty tub was a widely recognized literary allusion. In 1704 Jonathon Swift had written in *Tale of a Tub* that "seamen have a custom, when they meet a whale, to fling him out an empty tub by way of amusement, to divert him from laying violent hands upon the ship." Both Federalists and Antifederalists on occasion referred to Madison's proposals as "a tub to the whale," that is, insignificant amendments designed to divert attention away from more substantive amendments that would seriously weaken the powers of the federal government or alter the federal-state relationship.

An ambiguity in the meaning of the word, amendment, arose at the start of the ratification debate and continued throughout the contests. Support for amendments could indicate a desire either that personal liberties be protected or that fundamental changes be made in the balance of power between the state and federal governments and in the structure of the federal government, or both. In this essay I use amendment to refer to both types of proposals and alteration and bill of rights to distinguish between them. Alterations formed a clear majority of the amendments proposed by the states during the ratification process.

Electing the First Federal Congress

By the end of July 1788 eleven states had ratified the Constitution, but Madison and other leaders in the fight to strengthen the federal government during the 1780's had little time for celebration. Their critical, almost fatal, error at the federal Convention — the refusal to attach a bill of rights to the proposed Constitution — had cost dearly, most dramatically when New York Federalists were forced to join the dominant Antifederal majority in their state convention in an official call for a second federal convention, and when North Carolina refused to ratify without prior amendments.

August and September 1788 provided new threats: a group of New Yorkers attempted to unite Antifederalists up and down the coast; Congress deadlocked over where the first federal Congress should meet; and Pennsylvania Antifederalists called the first statewide political party convention in American history for the purpose of proposing amendments and selecting a slate of candidates to support them in the first House of Representatives. Federalists began to fear that Antifederalists might take control of the first Congress. George Washington lamented to Madison that "to be shipwrecked in sight of the port would be the severest of all possible aggravations to our misery."

Aside from the matter of amendments, no national issues arose during the first congressional election in the winter of 1788–89. Antifederalists did not fare well despite Federalist fears. Because of a general willingness on the part of most Antifederalists to give the new system a trial, an expectation of rights-related amendments, and partisan election laws in some states, voters elected six Federalists for every single Antifederalist.

The major contest — and the only one with national coverage — occurred in the Virginia Piedmont during January and February 1789. There, James Madison ran against his friend James Monroe, a moderate Antifederalist. Virginia's Fifth Congressional District had been carefully constructed by Patrick Henry to keep the nationally known and respected Madison out of the House of Representatives. Monroe advocated amendments to a sympathetic constituency, which had been led to believe that Madison was "dogmatically attached to the Constitution in every clause, syllable and letter." Such an opinion about Madison had a firm foundation, but it failed to acknowledge a shift that had gradually taken place in his thinking since he had characterized the subsequent amendments proposed by Massachusetts as a "blemish" and had convincingly argued in the Virginia ratifying convention against a federal bill of rights. Even as late as August 1788 he still desired a trial period of a few years to demonstrate what amendments the Constitution needed. North Carolina's refusal to ratify without amendments and the Antifederalists' resurgence as the autumn of 1788 approached converted Madison. It had taken him a year to accept the reality of the drastic mistake, which had been made at the federal Convention.

In private letters that he hoped would be published, Madison stressed that with the Constitution safely ratified, amendments could be considered. Specifically, he favored the proposal of amendments by Congress, rather than "essential rights." "In a number of other particulars," he wrote, "alterations are eligible either on their own account, or on account of those who wish for them." While clearly refuting the allegation that he opposed any amendments, his statement left vague how many and which alterations he would support.

In the balloting for representative, Madison defeated Monroe by a vote of 1,308 to 972. The fact that he had given his word during the campaign underlies all the reasons he later gave for supporting amendments. Virginia Antifederalists questioned the sincerity of Madison's conversion. George Mason emphasized that Madison would never have been elected without making some promises and noted that he had now become "the ostensible patron of amendments. Perhaps some milk and water propositions may be made . . . by way of throwing out a Tub to the Whale; but of important and substantial Amendments, I have not the least hope."

Madison's Unpopular Quest in Congress

When the first federal Congress assembled, Madison expected no great difficulty in getting the Federalist Congress to propose amendments to the states. On May 4 he gave notice that he would offer several in three weeks. He then agreed to two postponements to allow the revenue debate to proceed. Finally, informing his colleagues that he felt bound by honor and duty, on June 8 Madison moved that the House sit as a committee of the whole to receive and debate his proposals. But his colleagues quickly let him know that they did not consider the matter with equal urgency. They were not expressing opposition to the protection of civil liberties; on the contrary, almost all — even Madison's most vocal critics — held advanced libertarian ideas for their times. They had other reasons for opposing the debate. Amendments meant not only protection for civil liberty but potential alterations as well, and these would engender renewed debate over states' rights. In addition, members feared a public display of the deep sectional divisions within the young republic. Most Federalists, basking in their election victory, believed amendments unnecessary either as political stratagem or as protection for personal rights. Federalists called for postponement to allow a trial period for the new system. As Connecticut representative Roger Sherman, one of the most vocal opponents of amendments, expressed it, if the people had really wanted amendments they would have secured them prior to ratification. Antifederalists wanted postponement also, because they suggested Madison's proposals would fall far short of the alterations they sought. . . .

Madison's long and comprehensive speech converted neither the Federalists nor Antifederalists. Madison had "done his duty," South Carolina's Federalist William L. Smith smugly told the house, "and if he did not succeed, he was not to blame." Antifederalists again urged a postponement until the new government had been organized and the House could take up all the amendments of the states. The respect that many members felt for Madison, who acted as a sort of prime minister during the first session of Congress, resulted in the House referring his proposals to the committee as a whole.

Just before Madison made his proposals, Federalist representative George Clymer of Philadelphia speculated on whether Madison meant "merely a tub to the whale, a declaration about the press, liberty of conscience &c. or will suffer himself to be so far frightened with the antifederalism of his own state as to attempt to lop off essentials." After the speech Clymer summed up the view of almost everyone: Madison "has proved a tub" on amendments. Other Federalist representatives characterized Madison's proposals as innocent, nugatory, premature, and unnecessary. Boston's congressman, Fisher Ames, suggested they "may do some good towards quieting men, who attend to sounds only, and may get the mover some popularity which he wishes." Theodore Sedgwick of western Massachusetts thought the introduction of the "water gruel" proposals unwise and of no value politically. On and off the floor of Congress, both Ames and Sedgwick questioned Madison's motives and declared bills of rights to be of no constitutional importance.

Madison received a great deal of reaction to his proposals. "I like it as far as it goes; but I should have been for going further," wrote his mentor Jefferson. Others were less gentle. But letter also brought news he hoped to hear. Federalists and Antifederalists at both Philadelphia and Richmond approved. The news from North Carolina particularly encouraged him. Federalist Samuel Johnston, soon to be elected to the United States Senate, thought "a little flourish and dressing without injuring the substantial part or adding much to its intrinsic value, such as a pompous Declaration of Rights" might be enough to obtain ratification at the state's upcoming second convention.

Six weeks later, on July 21, Madison "begged" the House to take up his proposals. It spent the day debating whether to free the committee of the whole from its assignment and to appoint a select committee instead. Federalists could see no good purpose in discussing the subject below crowded public galleries, and so they established a select committee composed of a member from each state, despite the Antifederalist call for a public debate. The Committee, a majority of which was unsympathetic to amendments, reported back to the House a week later. It retained Madison's plan of incorporating the amendments into the body of the Constitution itself, rather than appending them to the document as committee member Roger Sherman urged.

The select committee tightened Madison's prose, rearranged his proposals, and considerably narrowed the absolute guarantees of religious freedom and the equal rights of conscience. Most prominently, the committee gutted the majestic natural-rights preamble, cutting out its declaration of the right of people to reform or change their government whenever it was found adverse or inadequate. Madison had proposed to include a statement concerning the purposes of government — the enjoyment of life and liberty, the acquisition and use of property, and the pursuit and obtaining of happiness and safety; but the committee eliminated this language. However, Sherman's attempt to limit Madison's absolute guarantee of the freedoms of speech and press by requiring that the words be decent failed in the committee. Madison, firmly attached to his own ideas if not to his own words, showed displeasure with the revision, although he admitted that perhaps some things had been changed for the better. Sherman thought the committee's proposals probably "harmless and satisfactory to those who are fond of Bills of rights." South Carolina congressman William L. Smith found them inoffensive and perhaps of some strategic benefit.

On August 13 the House debated whether to refer the select committee's report to the committee of the whole. Once again representatives from both parties urged postponement, but the House eventually yielded to Madison. The first motion set off a long debate as Roger Sherman again attempted without success to place any amendments at the end of the Constitution, rather than to incorporate them within the existing text.

From August 13 to 18 the committee of the whole considered each amendment individually. The high point of the debate took place on August 15, a sweltering Saturday, during an exchange between Federalists and Antifederalists. Led by Elbridge Gerry of Massachusetts, the other Antifederal speakers that day were South Carolinians Aedanus Burke, Thomas Tudor Tucker, and Thomas Sumter. Burke declared that the proposals before the amendments were "frothy and full of wind, formed only to please the palate; or they are like a tub thrown out to a whale, to secure the freight of the ship and its peaceful voyage." Madison responded to the attack. Had not Antifederalists told the people that they should oppose the Constitution until they secured these very rights? Had not the amendments he proposed been the ones most strenuously advocated by Antifederal leaders? Who was deceiving whom? he implied. Smith characterized the day's debate as more ill humored and rude than any other that had occurred in Congress.

Two more days of heated debate followed, during which there occurred the first known challenge to a duel among members of Congress. Speaker of the House Frederick A. Muhlenberg of Pennsylvania described the August 18 debate as the most heated and disorderly of the session to that point. At its close, the committee of the whole submitted the select committee's report to the House with only minor changes. Apparently none of the amendments had received the two-thirds majority needed to gain approval by the full House. Somehow Madison needed to garner more votes. President Washington, who had suggested in his inaugural address that Congress propose amendments promoting the rights of freemen without altering the system, provided Madison with written support. The president thought some of Madison's proposals unimportant, but "not foreseeing any evil consequences that can result from their adoption, they have my wishes for a favorable reception in both houses." Lukewarm though it might seem, the note probably influenced House Federalists to unite behind Madison's amendments. In addition, postponement or defeat of them at that stage of the process might provide Antifederalists with new ammunition by which to conduct a campaign for a second convention.

In securing Federalist votes to obtain the necessary two-thirds majority, Madison paid a two-part price: the House voted out the little that remained of his preamble, and it agreed to Sherman's motion that the amendments be placed at the end of the Constitution. Madison feared that this placement would lead to ambiguities about how far the original Constitution had been superseded by the amendments. Actually the change set a precedent for isolating amendments, broadened their role in constitutional law, and made it possible to point to a body of amendments known as the Bill of Rights. It is ironic that credit for this development belongs to a leading opponent of the Bill of Rights, Roger Sherman. . . .

On August 24 the House transmitted seventeen amendments to the Senate. The two Philadelphia representatives, George Clymer and Thomas Fitzsimons, advised their fellow townsman Senator Robert Morris that the Senate should "adopt the whole of them by lump as containing neither good or harm being perfectly innocent." Morris, who believed that the House had wasted valuable time on amendments and held Madison responsible, refused, and reportedly not only treated them contemptuously upon their arrival in the Senate but also joined several colleagues in an attempt at postponement until the next session. At the end of the Senate debate, he concluded that the amendments were merely a tub to the whale, while Senator Pierce Butler of South Carolina referred to them as "*milk and water*" propositions.

Virginia's two Antifederalist senators, Richard Henry Lee and William Grayson, faced insurmountable odds as they attempted to preserve and strengthen the House proposals. Complaining that Madison's amendments dealt with personal liberty alone, Grayson felt that Madison hoped to break the spirit of the Antifederal party by dividing it. Lee reported a debate over whether liberty of speech and freedom of the press should be struck from the amendments on the grounds that they tended only to encourage licentiousness among the people. One by one the Virginia senators vainly proposed the structural alterations recommended by their ratifying convention but ignored by Madison.

When the Senate completed work on the amendments on September 14, it had made twenty-six changes in the House proposals. In addition to tightening language, it had rearranged and compressed the seventeen articles into twelve and made significant changes in content. Struck from the House list were amendments forbidding the states from infringing upon certain rights of Americans, asserting separation of powers as a principle of the United States government, guaranteeing freedom of conscience, and exempting from military service those with religious objections. Also, the Senate weakened the guarantees of the religious liberty clause. Lee observed to Patrick Henry that the whole idea of subsequent rather than prior amendments to the Constitution had been little better than committing suicide, and Grayson reported to Henry that the proposed amendments were good for nothing and would do more harm than good.

Angered by the Senate changes, Madison reportedly declared that the amendments had lost their sedative virtue and that no amendments at all were better than those adopted by the Senate. Sherman and several congressmen who had reluctantly supported Madison welcomed the Senate's amending hand; consequently, when President Washington forwarded the twelve amendments to the states on October 2, most of the Senate changes remained. Would they satisfy Antifederalists as Madison hoped, or would there be demands by state legislatures for some or all of the additional amendments that the ratification conventions had proposed in 1788 and which Antifederalists had failed to secure in the first

Congress in 1789? If there were such demands, they might lead additional states to join Virginia and New York in petitioning Congress to call another constitutional convention.

A Quiet Ratification

Given the intensity of the congressional debate and all the public interest, which the question of amending the Constitution had raised during the campaign to ratify it and during the first congressional election, one would expect great contention over the ratification of Congress' twelve amendments. However, such controversy did not erupt for several reasons. First, Madison's political strategy proved successful. He won support for the Constitution from many Antifederalists who were not particularly concerned about the structural and states' rights amendments that their leaders sought. It had been a brilliant political move, perhaps the most important and successful in his career. As Thomas Jefferson expressed it to the Marquis de Lafayette in April 1790, "the opposition to our new constitution has almost totally disappeared. Some few indeed had gone to such lengths in their declarations of hostility that they feel it awkward perhaps to come over, but the amendments proposed by Congress have brought over almost all their followers."

A second reason for the absence of a debate over the ratification of the Bill of Rights related to the concept of federalism, the issue that had been central to American politics for twenty-five years. In implementing the Constitution, the first federal Congress refocused the debate over federalism in a fundamental way. The coalition that had supported a stronger federal government and secured ratification of the Constitution in 1788 achieved stunning legislative successes in the first session of the new Congress. Having attained its major goals and saved the ship of state from the Antifederal whale, the Federalist consensus split along sectional lines. Many Federalists began to move away from their earlier commitment to strengthening the federal government to a position that asserted the importance of protecting the rights of the states. James Madison, who in 1789 had blocked amendments designed to protect states' rights, quickly assumed for himself leadership of their cause in the early national era that lay ahead. . . .

By the end of the second session of the first Congress in 1790, twelve of the thirteen states had acted. Nine had ratified at least ten of the twelve amendments, Georgia had rejected all of them, and Massachusetts and Connecticut had failed to complete the adoption process. With ratification by ten states necessary to adopt the amendments, only one more approval was needed for the amendments to become part of the Constitution.

Virginia was the last state to act. More is known about the two-year ratification process there than in all the other states combined. In late September 1789 the state's Antifederal senators transmitted copies of the proposed amendments to the governor and speaker of the House of Delegates with remarkable covering letters. Expressing their grief, Lee and Grayson declared that they had done all they could do to procure the adoption of the "Radical" amendments proposed by the Virginia ratifying convention. They feared that the Constitution, if not further amended, would produce a consolidated empire, that is, one in which the states were either abolished or ignored. They predicted that if Congress did not propose further amendments, in a few years a sufficient number of state legislatures would demand a second federal convention, unless, of course, "a dangerous apathy should invade the public mind."

Not apathy, as Lee and Grayson feared, but satisfaction with Madison's proposals was what had seized the public mind in Virginia. Federalists reported that the senators' letters were not well received, even by some of the men who had voted against the Constitution at the ratifying convention. Although supported by Patrick Henry, the most powerful remaining Antifederal voice in the United States, a movement to postpone consideration of the amendments until 1790 failed. With defeat looming, Henry abandoned the fray and left Richmond for home. This proved unfortunate for Antifederalists, for at the end of the session a motion to ask Congress to adopt the rest of the Virginia convention's amendments failed by one vote when the speaker was called on to break a tie.

The most respected Antifederalist in Virginia, and perhaps in the nation, was George Mason, whose call for a bill of rights during the ratification process had been so influential. But Mason had been publicly silenced; not only was he an advocate of the rights-related amendments that Congress had proposed, but the very language of these additions had descended verbatim from his 1776 Virginia Declaration of Rights. Privately, however, he had something to say. "Unless some material amendments shall take place," Mason wrote his friend Secretary of State Thomas Jefferson, "I have always apprehended great Danger to the Rights and Liberty of our Country, and to that Cause, in Support of which I have so often had the Honour of acting in Concert with you, I fear in vain!" Jefferson responded that although he approved of the new government on the whole, he too wished to see additional amendments which would fix the federal government "more surely on a republican basis."

In November 1789 a solid majority of the Virginia House of Delegates voted to ratify all twelve amendments. . . .

. . . Secretary of State Thomas Jefferson informed the states on March 1, 1792, that the ten amendments which we call the Bill of Rights had become part of the Constitution. Considering the number and nature of the structural amendments that the states had called for during the process of considering the Constitution, it is perhaps ironic that the two congressionally proposed amendments most clearly structural (on apportionment and congressional salaries) were not adopted by a sufficient number of states.

In March and April 1939, as the United States began its celebration of the sesquicentennial of the Bill of Rights, Massachusetts, Georgia, and Connecticut belatedly ratified. By then it was obvious that both the constitutional role and the consecrated status of the federal Bill of Rights were due less to the foresight of the Founding Fathers than to the vigilance of a concerned citizenry, and especially to what Jefferson had called to Madison's attention in 1789 as an argument of "great weight" in favor of a bill of rights — "the legal check which it puts into the hands of the judiciary."

Questions for Discussion

1. How do you feel about Madison and the Federalists' advocacy of a bill of rights partly for pragmatic political reasons? Does this in any way diminish your esteem for the Bill of Rights? Why or why not?

2. Some Antifederalists were worried that a bill of rights would omit important civil liberties and that their absence would be taken as evidence that the American people were not entitled to them. How did the Bill of Rights in its final form address this dilemma?

3. Because the amendments comprising the Bill of Rights are concise and quite general in nature, the judiciary has had to interpret and apply them in very specific and challenging circumstances. Do you think that the judiciary has done its job effectively, modifying interpretations of certain civil liberties in light of changing historical circumstances? Or would we be better off if the meaning of these liberties had been set in a much more detailed and inflexible manner in the Bill of Rights?

3 Reflections on the Bicentennial of the United States Constitution

THURGOOD MARSHALL

In the introduction to an earlier case (selection #1), we noted that the moral center of the Founders was in large part influenced by the European Enlightenment. But what can we say about the Founders' apparent moral lapse concerning slavery? Can we apply our 21st-century approaches to the Founders' society? Some would say that the times were different then. The late Supreme Court Justice, Thurgood Marshall, would say that the continuance of slavery was a result of a compromise between the northeastern states and the southern states — a major injustice to thousands of humans who were held as slaves. Only the gradual and continuing evolution of the Constitution has brought the phrase "We the People" to more just light.

THE YEAR 1987 marks the 200th anniversary of the United States Constitution. A Commission has been established to coordinate the celebration. The official meetings, essay contests, and festivities have begun.

The planned commemoration will span three years, and I am told 1987 is "dedicated to the memory of the Founders and the document they drafted in Philadelphia." We are to "recall the achievements of our Founders and the knowledge and experience that inspired them, the nature of the government they established, its origins, its character, and its ends, and the rights and privileges of citizenship, as well as its attendant responsibilities."

Like many anniversary celebrations, the plan for 1987 takes particular events and holds them up as the source of all the very best that has followed. Patriotic feelings will surely swell, prompting proud proclamations of wisdom, foresight, and sense of justice shared by the framers and reflected in a written document now yellowed with age. This is unfortunate — not the patriotism itself, but the tendency for the celebration to oversimplify, and overlook the many other events that have been instrumental to our achievements as a nation. The focus of this celebration invites a complacent belief that the vision of those who debated and compromised in Philadelphia yielded the "more perfect Union" it is said we now enjoy.

I cannot accept this invitation, for I do not believe that the meaning of the Constitution was forever "fixed" at the Philadelphia Convention. Nor do I find the wisdom, foresight, and sense of justice exhibited by the framers particularly profound. To the contrary, the government they devised was defective from the start, requiring several amendments, a civil war, and momentous social transformation to attain the system of constitutional government, and its respect for the individual freedoms and human rights, that we hold as fundamental today. When contemporary Americans cite "The Constitution," they invoke a concept that is vastly different from what the framers barely began to construct two centuries ago.

For a sense of the evolving nature of the Constitution we need look no further than the first three words of the document's preamble: "We the People." When the Founding Fathers used this phrase in 1787, they did not have in mind the majority of America's citizens. "We the People" included, in the words of the framers, "the whole number of free persons." On a matter so basic as the right to vote, for example, Negro slaves were excluded, although they were counted for representational purposes — at three-fifths each. Women did not gain the right to vote for over a hundred and thirty years.

These omissions were intentional. The record of the framers' debates on the slave question is especially clear: the Southern states acceded to the demands of the New England states for giving Congress broad power to regulate commerce, in exchange for the right to continue the slave trade. The economic interests of the regions coalesced: New Englanders engaged in the "carrying trade" would profit from transporting slaves from Africa as well as goods produced in America by slave labor. The perpetuation of slavery ensured the primary source of wealth in the Southern states.

Despite this clear understanding of the role slavery would play in the new republic, use of the words "slave" and "slavery" was carefully avoided in the original document. Political representation in the lower House of Congress was to be based on the population of "free Persons" in each state, plus three-fifths of all "other Persons." Moral principles against slavery, for those who had them, were compromised, with no explanation of the conflicting principles for which the American Revolutionary War had ostensibly been fought: the self-evident truths "that all men are created equal, that they are endowed by their Creator with certain unalienable Rights, that among these are Life, Liberty, and the Pursuit of Happiness."

It was not the first such compromise. Even these ringing phrases from the Declaration of Independence are filled with irony, for an early draft of what became that declaration assailed the King of England for suppressing legislative attempts to end the slave trade and for encouraging slave rebellions. The final draft adopted in 1776 did not contain this criticism. And so again at the Constitutional Convention eloquent objections to the institution of slavery went unheeded, and its opponents eventually consented to a document which laid a foundation for the tragic events that were to follow.

Pennsylvania's Governeur Morris provides an example. He opposed slavery and the counting of slaves in determining the basis for representation in Congress. At the Convention he objected that

> The inhabitant of Georgia [or] South Carolina who goes to the coast of Africa, and in defiance of the most sacred laws of humanity tears away his fellow creatures from their dearest connections and damns them to the most cruel bondages, shall have more votes in a government instituted for protection of the rights of mankind, than the Citizen of Pennsylvania or New Jersey who views with a laudable horror, so nefarious a practice.

And yet Governeur Morris eventually accepted the three-fifths accommodation. In fact, he wrote the final draft of the Constitution, the very document the bicentennial will commemorate.

As a result of the compromise, the right of the Southern states to continue importing slaves was extended, officially, at least until 1808. We know that it actually lasted a good deal longer, as the framers possessed no monopoly on the ability to trade moral principles for self-interest. But they nevertheless set an unfortunate example. Slaves could be imported, if the commercial interests of the North were protected. To make the compromise even more palatable, customs duties would be imposed at up to ten dollars per slave as a means of raising public revenues.

No doubt it will be said, when the unpleasant truth of the history of slavery in America is mentioned during this bicentennial year, that the Constitution was a product of its times, and embodied a compromise which, under other circumstances, would not have been made. But the effects of the framers' compromise have remained for generations. They arose from the contradiction between guaranteeing liberty and justice to all, and denying both to Negroes.

The original intent of the phrase "We the People," was far too clear for any ameliorating construction. Writing for the Supreme Court in 1857, Chief Justice Taney penned the following passage in the *Dred Scott* case, on the issue of whether, in the eyes of the framers, slaves were "constituent members of the sovereignty," and were to be included among "We the People":

> We think they are not, and that they are not included, and were not intended to be included . . . They had for more than a century before been regarded as beings of an inferior order, and altogether unfit to associate with the white race . . . ; and so far inferior, that they had no rights which the white man was bound to respect; and that the negro might justly and lawfully be reduced to slavery for his benefit . . . . [A]ccordingly, a negro of the African race was regarded . . . as an article of property, and held, and bought and sold as such. . . . [No] one seems to have doubted the correctness of the prevailing opinion of the time.

And so, nearly seven decades after the Constitutional Convention, the Supreme Court reaffirmed the prevailing opinion of the framers regarding the rights of Negroes in America. It took a bloody civil war before the thirteenth amendment could be adopted to abolish slavery, though not the consequences slavery would have for future Americans.

While the Union survived the civil war, the Constitution did not. In its place arose a new, more promising basis for justice and equality, the fourteenth amendment, ensuring protection of the life, liberty, and property of *all* persons against deprivations without due process, and guaranteeing equal protection of the laws. And yet almost another century would pass before any significant recognition was obtained of the rights of black Americans to share equally even in such basic opportunities as education, housing, and employment, and to have their votes counted, and counted equally. In the meantime, blacks joined America's military to fight its wars and invested untold hours working in its factories and on its farms, contributing to the development of this country's magnificent wealth and waiting to share in its prosperity.

What is striking is the role legal principles have played throughout America's history in determining the condition of Negroes. They were enslaved by law, emancipated by law, disenfranchised and segregated by law; and finally, they have begun to win equality by law. Along the way, new constitutional principles have emerged to meet the challenges of a changing society. The progress has been dramatic, and it will continue.

The men who gathered in Philadelphia in 1787 could not have envisioned these changes. They could not have imagined, nor would they have accepted, that the document they were drafting would one day be constructed by a Supreme Court to which had been appointed a woman and the descendent of an African slave. "We the People" no longer enslaves, but the credit does not belong to the framers. It belongs to those who refused to acquiesce in outdated notions of "liberty," "justice," and "equality," and who strived to better them.

And so we must be careful, when focusing on the events which took place in Philadelphia two centuries ago, that we not overlook the momentous events which followed, and thereby lose our proper sense of perspective. Otherwise, the odds are that for many Americans the bicentennial celebration will be little more than a blind pilgrimage to the shrine of the original document now stored in a vault in the National Archives. If we seek, instead, a sensitive understanding of the Constitution's inherent defects and its promising evolution through 200 years of history, the celebration of the "Miracle at Philadelphia" will, in my view, be a far more meaningful and humbling experience. We will see that the true miracle was not the birth of the Constitution, but its life, a life nurtured through two turbulent centuries of our own making, and a life embodying much good fortune that was not.

Thus, in this bicentennial year, we may not all participate in the festivities with flag-waving fervor. Some may more quietly commemorate the suffering, struggle, and sacrifice that has triumphed over much of what was wrong with the original document, and observe the anniversary with hopes not realized and promises not fulfilled. I plan to celebrate the bicentennial of the Constitution as a living document, including the Bill of Rights and the other amendments protecting individual freedoms and human rights.

Questions for Discussion

1. What do you make of the Constitution? Do you see it as a considerable accomplishment in its historical setting, or do you see it instead as just a serviceable creation that happened to adapt and improve over the course of American history?

2. The Constitution was a practical political compromise, but it also was the handiwork of idealists. Were the Founders accurate in their belief that

the Constitution could not have come into being without the acceptance of the institution of slavery? If so, were they right to "make a deal," or should they have stood their ground and rejected such a compromise — even at the expense of the ratification of the Constitution?

3.   Is Justice Marshall mindful enough of the political realities of the setting in which the Framers created the Constitution? Does he give them enough credit for their handiwork, or is he too critical of them?

4 Where Have All the Great Men Gone?

RICHARD D. BROWN

Do certain elements of a society produce great leaders? Are men and women shaped by their challenges while in public office? In this selection, Richard Brown makes two lists of five characteristics: One list includes knowledge, genius, judgment, courage, and moral character — the criteria for leadership of the elite class of the young republic. The second list, competitiveness, personal ambition, experience, media visibility, and electioneering performance, Brown notes, seems to reflect a more modern set of criteria for attaining the position of leadership. Have the great leaders really gone?

THERE IS NO CLEAR CONSENSUS on what constitutes greatness, nor are there any objective criteria for measuring it — but when we look at holders of high public offices and at the current field of candidates, we know it is missing. Some of our leaders are competent, articulate, engaging, and some are honest and honorable. But greatness is missing.

The leaders of the early republic — George Washington, Thomas Jefferson, John Adams, Benjamin Franklin, Alexander Hamilton, and John Marshall — set the standard for greatness. Since their day only Abraham Lincoln and Franklin D. Roosevelt have attained equivalent stature. Why has mediocrity come to prevail where meritocracy once ruled? Where have all the great men gone?

This question is more complicated than it may first appear, and some will argue that the issues it raises are false and ahistorical, since responses to the question must be subjective. Indeed, some will say that to pose the question is to retreat into romantic mythology where the founders of the republic become the heroic figures of a "golden age." These objections cannot be ignored.

It has been said that a statesman is nothing but a dead politician. From the time we are children we are taught not to speak ill of the dead, and in public rhetoric it is common to elevate them. In our own time admiration for John F. Kennedy exemplifies this phenomenon, and earlier in this century the reputation of the assassinated President William McKinley enjoyed a similar glorification that only gradually ebbed away. Nostalgia distorts historical perceptions, a fact that has nourished revisionist historiography for generations. In fact, revisionism in American historical writing began with the early twentieth-century discovery that the Founding Fathers were flesh-and-blood politicians, and however obvious that "discovery" now appears, it remains a vital corrective to "golden age" thinking.

Yet even admitting all of this, scholars who have closely scrutinized the major leaders of the early republic continue to be enormously impressed. The array of talented and devoted individuals is awesome. In Massachusetts, for instance, John and Samuel Adams, Elbridge Gerry and John Hancock, Robert Treat Paine and James and Joseph Warren, immediately come to mind, as well as a dozen less exalted figures — a James Bowdoin, a Henry Knox, a Benjamin Lincoln, a James Sullivan. We need not agree that they all were truly great, but if we compare them with the present incumbents, the sense of loss and deprivation is overwhelming.

At the end of the eighteenth century as today, political leaders were chiefly drawn from the white male population aged forty to sixty years. Leaving aside questions of wealth and education, Massachusetts in 1790 possessed about thirty thousand such people, the United States as a whole some two-hundred and fifty thousand. Today [in 1984] there are eighty times that number nationwide, twenty million white men aged forty to sixty years. And the total voting population of that age is forty-four million. Considered in light of these figures, the ability of the early republic to generate so many talented officeholders cannot be dismissed as mere patriotic mythology. We are talking about an actual fact.

Biographies cannot provide an explanation. The almost routine emergence of such able leaders was a social phenomenon, and to understand it we must examine the society that produced them. What were the conditions that created this political pattern, and when and why did it recede?

The folklore of politics teaches us that great events produce great men, and we can all think of examples where great events ennobled public figures who had previously and accurately been viewed as undistinguished. In 1932 the journalist Walter Lippmann observed that Franklin D. Roosevelt was "an amiable Boy Scout . . . a pleasant man who, without any important qualifications for the office, would very much like to be

President." Unquestionably, the crises of the Depression and World War II elevated Roosevelt's leadership. Had he served during the 1920s, there is no reason to believe his Presidency would be memorable.

Yet this phenomenon is not inevitable. Great events and great challenges produce George McClellans and George Wallaces as well as George Washingtons. No natural law requires societies to assign their most talented members to positions of public trust in times of crises. To understand the nature of how we actually do select our leaders, we must begin by examining the systems of recruiting and advancing public officials within a republican government.

I believe that the United States currently operates a peculiar, debased form of meritocracy, which has five major attributes: first, access to high office is extremely competitive; second, keen personal ambition for power and recognition is necessary to propel people into the competition and keep them there; third, the system calls for a record of experience in public or quasi-public affairs; fourth, it requires visibility through media exposure; finally, what these four elements point to is the fifth characteristic of our system of recruitment and advancement — electioneering performance. The ability to perform in election contests, to go out tirelessly day after day in search of support and to win it from people of diverse characteristics — this is the ultimate criterion.

This system of political advancement operates directly through the electorate and indirectly through elites that recognize the ultimate authority of the ballot box. Because the electorate and the elites are so diverse, electioneering on a national scale or in any large state requires tireless campaigning to persuade people from a multitude of different backgrounds, often with directly conflicting interests, to look with hopeful anticipation on a single person. Chameleonlike, the candidate must appeal to boardroom and back room, fans of symphonies and Super Bowls. From the standpoint of electioneering, our current system is meritocractic, but the attributes that lead to success at the ballot box often seem to assure mediocrity in public office.

It was not always thus. At the outset of the republic, recruitment and advancement operated differently. First of all, the electorate was confined to white, male property-holders who had been schooled in the deferential politics of the colonial era. This was an electorate that expected political leaders to be men of wealth and education, not ordinary people like themselves. Moreover, in choosing candidates, voters were accustomed to supporting men whom they knew face-to-face or through local reputation. If they voted for a stranger, it was usually because that stranger carried the endorsement of a trusted member of the local elite. As far as the electorate was concerned, the role of candidates themselves in seeking office was largely passive.

The key process of nominating candidates was dominated by layers of local, state, and national elites. Candidates were selected by their peers, people who had witnessed them in action for years and who knew first-hand their strengths and weaknesses. Whatever the office in question, relatively homogeneous groups of incumbents and their associates selected candidates from among their own number. While the system was open to new men, and choices required approval at the polls, it had a distinctly oligarchic flavor. High esteem among the peer group was a prerequisite for major elective offices.

This brief comparison between the present system, where electoral popularity is the ultimate criterion, and the early republic, where peer-group approval was paramount, helps to focus our analysis, but it does not answer the question of the disappearing great men. Though it might be tempting to offer a simple elitist explanation, this would be worse than inadequate; it would be wrong. Historically the records of elite selection processes are replete with instances of incompetence, corruption, and tyranny — and mediocrity. Whether operated by Byrd in Virginia, Daley in Chicago, or Tweed in New York City, the record of oligarchic rule inside the United States, as elsewhere, is not synonymous with meritocracy. The central question then is not techniques of recruitment and advancement *per se*; it is the values that animate the process.

During the first generation of the republic there was a clear consensus among leading men in all parts of the nation regarding fundamental political values. This consensus was grounded on the classical models that were central to the curricula at all the colonial colleges, from William and Mary in Virginia to Harvard in Massachusetts. Ideals of citizenship and public office were drawn from the history of the Roman republic. First of all, private, personal virtue was a prerequisite to public virtue and hence a requirement for high office. The object of political leadership was to implement the general public good, and in order to perceive and pursue it, leaders must be men of superior wisdom, energy, initiative, and moral stature. The people were not their guides, they were their charges, to be led along paths selected by the leaders. An aristocracy of merit — Jefferson called it a "natural aristocracy" — should rule.

In practical politics this classical model dictated that the man should never seek the office, the office should seek the man. The historical figure of Cincinnatus, who had been called from his plow to lead his people, was the ideal type. In our Revolutionary days, George Washington and Israel Putnam, among others, were presented in this mold. . . .

The difficulty of any merit system is how to measure merit. Early republican leaders sought the judgments of informed gentlemen, relying on their discretion as to whether merit was "eminently distinguished and generally acknowledged." Here personal acquaintance — "connections" — was often crucial, and the meritocractic possibilities of patronage were developed.

At the core of the system trust ruled. Assessments of character and abilities were necessarily subjective, so those who selected candidates for civil and military office had to rely on the testimony of their peers. John Adams's correspondence as a member of the board of war illustrates the system's values and the way it worked. To his old law clerk, Adams wrote in August 1776: "I am . . . determined to pursue this Correspondence, until I can obtain a perfect Knowledge of the Characters of our Field Officers." Of one man Adams asserted: "His Genius is equal to any one of his Age. His Education is not inferior. So far I can Say of my own Knowledge"; but before Adams could recommend promotion, he needed to know more about the candidate's "Morals, his Honour, and his Discretion." On the same day Adams complained in another letter to a colleague that Massachusetts

> continues to act, the most odd Surprising and unaccountable Part, respecting Officers. They have a most wonderful Faculty of finding out Persons for Generals and Colonells of whom no Body ever heard before. Let me beg of you, in Confidence to give me your candid and explicit opinion, of the Massachusetts General and Field Officers, and point out such as have any Education, Erudition, Sentiment, Reflection, Address or other Qualification or Accomplishment excepting Honour and Valour for Officers in high Rank. Who and What is General Fellows? Who and What is General Brickett? . . .
>
> If there are any officers, young or old, among the Massachusetts Forces who have Genius, Spirit, Reflection, Science, Literature, and Breeding, do for the Lands sake, and the Armys sake, and the Province sake let me know their Names, Places of Abodes and Characters.

Adams was a part of a national talent search, and he begged for candid assessments of individuals. The reports he received from political acquaintances in the Northern states reveal the application of meritocractic principles to the process of advancing people according to known connections. From New York a friend of Adams, a lawyer, now serving as a Continental officer, provided him with these ratings of the Massachusetts colonels:

WHITCOMB: has no Trace of an Officer, his Men under no Government

REED: A good Officer not of the most extensive Knowledge but far from being low or despicable . . .

LITTLE: A Midling Officer and of tolerable Genius, not great

SERJEANT: has a pretty good Character but I have no Acquaintance

GLOVER: is said to be a good Officer but am not acquainted

HUTCHINSON: An easy good Man not of great Genius

BALEY: is Nothing

BALDWIN: a Personable Man but not of the first Character

LEARNED: Was a good officer, is old, Superanuated and Resigned

GREATON: An excellent Disciplinarian his Courage has been questioned, but I don't know with what Justice

BOND: I don't know him

PATTERSON: A Good Officer of a liberal Education, ingenious and Sensible.

The key, qualifications are knowledge, "genius," and judgment in addition to the courage and moral character that were prerequisites.

For the highest positions, such as major general, and later for President, much more was wanted. In August 1776 Adams reflected on the essential qualities for the highest of offices. Such a person, Adams believed: "should be possessed of a very extensive Knowledge of Science, and Literature, Men and Things. A Citizen of a free Government, be Should be Master of the Laws and Constitution, least he injure fundamentally those Rights which he professes to defend. He Should have a keen Penetration and a deep Discernment of the Tempers, Natures, and Characters of Men. He Should have an Activity, and Diligence, Superiour to all Fatigue. He should have a Patience and Self Government, Superior to all Flights and Transports of Passion. He Should have a Candour and Moderation, above all Prejudices, and Partialities. His Views should be large enough to comprehend the whole System of the Government and the Army. . . . His Benevolence and Humanity, his Decency, Politeness and Civility, Should ever predominate in his Breast. He should be possessed of a certain . . . order, Method, and Decision, Superior to all Perplexity and Confusion in Business. There is in Such a Character, whenever and wherever it appears, a decisive Energy, which hurries away before it, all Difficulties, and leaves to the World of Mankind no Leisure, or opportunity to do any Thing towards it, but Admire, it." From the perspective of 1776, Adams's idealism was not idle fantasy. Already the Continental Congress and the republic had found one such individual in George Washington.

In order to discern such qualities one could only resort to known men. Speaking of the selection of officers in October 1775, Adams remarked that "Men of Honour cannot appoint Gentlemen whom they don't know. . . . Nor can they pay a Regard to any Recommendation of Strangers, to the Exclusion of Persons whom they know." Personal knowledge and the recommendations of acquaintances — personal connections — were crucial. Traditionally these were the mechanisms of patronage, where friends and relatives sponsored each other's promotion, with merit no more than a secondary consideration. In the Revolutionary republic at its best, however, the new idealism transformed old, quasi-oligarchic practices into a screen for talent, wisdom, and character. . . .

Actually, Gordon S. Wood, the leading authority on the effort to create the Constitution of 1787, believes that one of its central objectives was to screen out the direct influence of the people from the government, enabling the elites to select from among their own number the people they believed were best qualified to guide the United States. The provisions of the Constitution prescribing the selection of the principal public officials clearly limited the impact of popular elections. The President was to be chosen by an Electoral College, and failing a majority there, by the House of Representatives. The members of the United States Senate were to be elected by the individual state legislatures. The only popularly elected officers would be members of the House of Representatives, but since their constituencies were so large (at least forty thousand people), it was believed that only prominent men of proven abilities would possess the visibility and wide acquaintance necessary for election.

The conviction that men of merit according to upper-class standards must dominate public office was a consistent theme in the Federalist administrations of Washington and Adams, but the election of 1800 and the ensuing party competition between Jeffersonians and Federalists pointed in a new direction. After Jefferson took office, even the majority of Federalists were prepared to give the people what they wanted, tailoring policy to popular wishes instead of to abstract principles of the public good. While it is hard to fix a precise date for the demise of the system of political recruitment and advancement that produced so many great men, it was weakening in the early decades of the new century, and in the presidential election of 1828 its utter defeat is evident.

As President, John Quincy Adams was a political anachronism. His election in 1824 was the only case where the electoral process set up in 1787 to assure the best choice in case of deadlock had actually been employed. When no one commanded a majority in the Electoral College, the selection of the President fell to the House of Representatives. Here his fellow candidate Henry Clay decided that Adams would make a better President than Andrew Jackson, who had won a plurality of popular votes. Whatever Clay's motives, by following this course he directly repudiated the popular vote as well as the instructions of his own Kentucky legislature. The system of elite selection worked, for Adams was indeed superbly qualified for the highest office according to the classical republican canons of education, experience, intelligence, energy, and moral stature. But he lacked popularity and the willingness to seek it. In 1828 he and the meritocractic system he symbolized were defeated.

John Quincy Adams saw clearly what was going on. In his memoirs he confided: "Electioneering for the Presidency has spread its contagion to the President himself. . . . One of the most remarkable peculiarities of the present time is that the principal leaders of the political parties are travelling about the country from State to State, and holding forth, like Methodist preachers, hour after hour, to assembled multitudes, under the broad canopy of heaven." Adams would not lift a finger to pursue reelection. He ignored his own party's pleas for help and even refused to state that he wished to be elected. Like a caricature of the classical ideal, he stood for office in silence.

Meanwhile, professional politicians flocked to Andrew Jackson because his military reputation made him famous and popular. Jackson's career lent itself to magnification, and strategists organized parties, parades, and house-to house canvassing to turn out the Jackson vote in 1828 on behalf of a common man's crusade. Though Andrew Jackson was a person of unusual ability and genuine achievement, he was elected because he appeared to symbolize popular feelings. In 1840, when the Whigs successfully ran the aged and obscure William Henry Harrison as a Jackson look-alike in the "hard-cider," "log-cabin," "Tippecanoe and Tyler too" campaign, the absolute corruption of the selection process was evident. Mediocrity was more popular than meritocracy, and henceforth it would be qualities associated with electioneering success that would determine recruitment and advancement.

Elites still selected candidates in party caucuses and conventions, but they measured their choices against popular preferences and party loyalty. In an age when sentiment was supplanting reason in religion and the arts, when egalitarianism was destroying the legitimacy of natural as well as hereditary aristocracy, the values embodied in the classical republican ideal lost out in the race for popularity. During the Civil War the Boston brahmin historian Francis Parkman probed the fundamental issues: "Our ship is among breakers, and we look about us for a pilot. An endangered nation seeks a leader worthy of itself. . . . In a struggle less momentous it found such leaders. . . . Out of three millions, America found a Washington, an Adams, a Franklin, a Jefferson, a Hamilton; out of twenty millions she now finds none whose stature can compare with these. She is strong in multitudes, swarming with brave men, instinct with eager patriotism. But she fails in that which multitudes cannot supply, those master minds, the lack of which the vastest aggregate of mediocrity can never fill. . . . Where are they? Why is mediocrity in our high places, and the race of our statesmen so dwindled? . . . The people have demanded equality, not superiority, and they have had it: men of the people, that is to say, men in no way raised above the ordinary level of humanity. In degrading its high offices, the nation has weakened and degraded itself."

Ironically, these words were written just as the nation was about to discover the greatness of Abraham Lincoln. Yet the fact of Lincoln's ultimate stature does not diminish the cogency of Parkman's analysis. Lincoln was in fact elected as the common man incarnate. The fact that he subsequently displayed the superior qualities of wisdom, rectitude, and courage was accidental. His immediate predecessors in the highest office, Buchanan, Pierce, Fillmore, and Taylor, like his immediate successors, Johnson, Grant, Hayes, and Garfield, testify that the remarkable qualities Lincoln possessed were not requirements for nomination or election.

Today's political system remains dynamic, and it has departed from that of the nineteenth century in a number of important ways. Senators are now elected directly by the voters. Primary elections for state and national offices have partially supplanted party conventions, and candidates appeal to voters directly through radio and television. Yet these developments represent logical extensions of the popular, egalitarian spirit that animated the nineteenth century. . . .

Overall we are more comfortable with people not much different from ourselves. Sen. Roman L. Hruska elevated this observation to a statement of principle in defending President Nixon's nomination of G. Harold Carswell for the Supreme Court in 1970. Hruska said that he would support Carswell "even if he were mediocre," since "there are a lot of mediocre judges and people and lawyers, and they are entitled to a little representation, aren't they?" Hruska's only error lies in supposing that mediocrity is not already well represented in the high councils of the nation.

Hruska's statement is embarrassing because normally we do not like to admit our suspicion of superiority. In the end, however, we regularly elect plausible, supple politicians who have the patience for endless campaigning and who are appealing rather than admirable.

Still, greatness is not absolutely ruled out. At special historical moments a highest common denominator may be discovered and, as with
Lincoln and Roosevelt, greatness may luckily emerge. But greatness, of
course, is an exceptional phenomenon; even under the best conditions
the odds must always be against it. By selecting leaders as we do, we
lengthen those odds dramatically. In order to better our chances, a revolution in our system of recruiting and selecting leaders would be required,
as well as a revolution in values. We would have to admit that the people,
who glimpse candidates only momentarily from a distance, and through
the filters of the media, do not have the capacity to judge who is fit for
office. We would have to reject the democratic egalitarian ethos under
which our political system has been operating for over a century.

I do not advise revolution. The great men who led in founding our
republic would offer the same counsel. After all, they made the Revolution
for the sake of liberty through law, and they created the Constitution
because history had taught them it was dangerous to rely on the individual
merit or virtue of rulers. They placed their faith in constitutional government, arranging power so as to rely on laws, not men. They believed
that, in the long run, this gave the best hope for freedom. Their greatest
fear was not the mediocrity and inadequacy of leaders, it was the apathy,
ignorance, and petty selfishness of the people. When public morals became
corrupt, they warned, liberty would languish.

Perhaps their warning is relevant for our own time. Our longing
for great men and women to lead us out of the wilderness is, in classical
republican terms, a sign of lassitude, of the corruption that encourages
demagogues and leads to tyranny. Informed by history, we should understand that the circumstances that led to the sparkling era when personal
greatness and high public office coincided were unique, and exceptional.
To expect greatness in public office, to anticipate a new meritocracy that
can solve our problems, is a fantasy. The public interest and the safety of
free government are better served by an alert, informed citizenry seeking
to promote the common good. Whether that, too, is fantasy, only time
will tell.

Questions for Discussion

1. Is there such a thing as a natural aristocracy? What determines at any
particular moment in history whether a certain type of person is more fit
to lead and govern than other people?

2.   Does the mass media today "screen" candidates the way elites and political parties did in the past?

3.   Can politicians today stick to their convictions and win elections by "telling it like it is"? Or, have we reached the point at which candidates can build broad electoral coalitions only by trying to be "all things to all people"?

PART TWO

DECISIONS

5 Washington: The Indispensable Man

JAMES THOMAS FLEXNER

Leadership can take many forms, and if there has been any American who demonstrated most forms of leadership, it was George Washington. Here, in James Thomas Flexner's passage, Washington demonstrates a particular form of leadership. With the Revolutionary War almost over, General Washington faced new crises: an army unpaid and restless, conspirators eager to co-opt his command. But the Commander in Chief stood firm. Considering himself more a civilian in arms than professional soldier, Washington provided a powerful moment in leadership by example.

HE INTENDED SOON to join his army beside the Hudson, but he was held in the capital for four months [in 1781]. The basic military problems were now more than ever grounded in the civilian sphere. Despite the still powerful British presence, there was a general feeling that the Revolution was as good as won. This portended so much more neglect of the already extremely neglected army that, should Clinton or his government decide to undertake another serious military effort, the Continental force might be helpless. And there was also the possibility that the American soldiers, embittered by indifference to their needs, would themselves destroy, in one way or another, the freedom for which they had fought.

The financial difficulties — no money available to give bounties to or to support and pay the existing army — were symptoms of a more serious rot. The thirteen colonies had been driven into close cooperation by a crisis which gave them the alternatives Benjamin Franklin had so aptly described: if they did not hang together, they would hang separately. But even on the heights of the crisis, the states had argued for years before they could agree on Articles of Confederation, which did little more than create a loose alliance. Now that the crisis seemed to be fading, the states were becoming increasingly indifferent to the Continental Congress and the combined effort it fostered.

Under Washington's urging, the Congress appropriated for the next campaign eight million dollars. Although this was barely enough to keep the core of an army in the field and although Washington wrote hortatory letters to the various governors, the states did not supply Congress with money enough to pay even the interest on already outstanding debts.

The obvious and necessary solution was that the central body be allowed to raise money in its own right. Washington's hopes and the anticipations of the troops came to depend on the proposition that Congress be empowered to collect customs duties. However, the Articles of Confederation had so rigorously preserved local sovereignty that federal taxation could only be authorized through unanimous agreement of all the states. As winter dragged into the spring of 1782 and on towards autumn, the matter was considered by the various state legislatures. Favorable votes were reported, but the fact remained that if any laggard voted no or refused to act, the army would surely not receive its past and present dues. . . .

Washington did his best to think of ways of amusing his troops in idleness. He sent his officers home on long furloughs, urged the men to vie with each other in decorating their huts and their hats. Encouraging one of New England's favorite sports, he wrote that religious discourses "must afford the most pure and rational entertainment for any serious and well-disposed mind." But he noted that the dissatisfaction was taking on a new and ominous note. Formerly, the officers had tried to quiet the men. Now they were leading the protests.

The situation was already dangerous enough when Congress decided to cut expenses by reducing the number of regiments in a way that would demobilize many officers. However, no provision was made for giving them any pay, although some were owed (as Washington noted) for "four, five, or perhaps six years." A promise of pensions previously made at a dark moment in the war showed no likelihood of being honored. To officials in Philadelphia, Washington wrote bitterly that the demobilized officers would depart "goaded by a thousand stings of reflection on the past and of anticipation on the future . . . soured by penury and what they call the ingratitude of the public, involved in debts, without one farthing of money to carry them home, after having spent the flowers of their days, and many of them their patrimonies, in establishing the freedom and independence of their country, and suffered everything human nature is capable of enduring on this side of death. . . . I cannot avoid apprehending that a train of evils will follow of a very serious and distressing nature."

The summer of 1782 passed in frustrating doldrums. Washington hoped to spend the following winter at Mount Vernon, recruiting his strength and attending to his neglected private concerns. But when the time for departure came, he felt that the temper of the army was such that he could not leave.

The plight of the officers who had already been demobilized could not help seeming frighteningly prophetic: when no longer needed to protect the civilian population, every soldier, all obligations forgotten, would also be sent home in penury. It seemed to follow that while the troops were still together, they should take the steps necessary to make sure that the civilian authorities would give them the pay that was owed and secure to them the pensions that had been voted them. The Massachusetts regiments sent a delegation to their own government, only to be shunted on to the Congress. But Massachusetts was delinquent (as were all the other states) in meeting her part of the quota that would help make Congress solvent enough to pay the army.

Over campfires in the chill autumn, warmed sometimes with rum, the officers fingered the hilts of their swords and talked of taking the law in their own hands. Only by the most intense persuasion did Washington channel the discontent into a petition to Congress. There had been petitions before, but this one was accompanied by a not-too-subtle threat. It was to be presented by a committee of three high officers who were to stay in Philadelphia until it became clear whether justice would be done or not. If not, the army would consider more decisive action.

Since Congress's requisitions to the states were continuing to fall on deaf ears, everything depended on the fate of the amendment to the Articles that would allow Congress to collect its own taxes. Hardly had the military committee reached the capital when adverse votes of both Rhode Island and Virginia carried the amendment to defeat. The committee angrily warned Congress that the soldiers "were verging on a state which we are told will drive wise men mad." But Congress, being bankrupt, could do nothing.

Almost every revolution in the history of the world, however idealistically begun, had ended in tyranny. The American Revolution had now reached its moment of major political crisis.

Now that independence seemed at hand, the state leaders felt their own urgency: it should be made clear, for the impending future, that the United States was not one nation but thirteen. But state autonomy was not the basis on which the war had been fought. It had been necessary to create a Continental Congress and a Continental Army, and also to incur

Continental debts. These debts were not only to the soldiers. Congress also owed much to civilians. There was the currency it had printed, which should be honored, even if at less than face value. There were certificates of indebtedness: bonds and various acknowledgments of loans; paper Washington had, when deprived of more specific means of payment, given to farmers and wagoners; the multitudinous other kinds of paper emitted by a bankrupt government scrambling for existence. Since the poor had been unable to wait, they had usually sold their certificate of indebtedness to speculators for a fraction of the true value. The paper had thus found its way into the hands of large operators. The financial community was as deeply involved as were the soldiers in the national obligations which the states were trying, as they delicately looked the other way, to sweep under the rug.

The fact that the army and the ablest, most prosperous businessmen were being similarly defrauded opened a promising field for common action. The members of the military committee that had been sent to Philadelphia conferred with the leading financiers, particularly Robert and Governeur Morris. It was agreed that the only protection for the creditors, whether civilians or soldiers, was the military strength of the army. The army should, even if peace were declared, refuse to go home until the states agreed to a system by which all federal debts could be paid. If necessary, violence should be threatened to achieve what was basically required: a strong central government that could protect the rights of its creditors. Should military force be used to reform the state legislatures, that would, it was said (and probably often believed), be only a temporary expedient until the necessary changes were achieved. Then the government would be returned to the people. So it was argued. The modern reader will see being groomed and saddled the horses of fascism.

The road ahead seemed clear except for one serious potential barrier: George Washington. Would the national hero be willing to countenance a movement to use the army as a political force? And if he refused to go along, could he be pushed aside?

The conspirators agreed that the ground should be prepared for getting rid of Washington and finding another leader. However, it would be infinitely better to persuade Washington. Washington's former aide, Alexander Hamilton, now a congressman from New York, announced that he knew how to handle the General. He would undertake the mission.

Washington's role in the Revolution had always been more than military. After electing him Commander in Chief, the members of Congress had committed themselves to the cause by committing themselves to support him. And their need for his help had proved to be great. As a legislative body entrusted with all executive functions, the Congress had tried to administer the war and the army by setting up committees of its members. There were soon more committees than the members had time for, and the method was at best cumbersome. Because the committees so often failed to act, Washington was continually forced, in order to keep his army alive, into himself making decisions with much wider implications than the purely military. And on several occasions when Congress became frightened by British successes, the legislators officially dumped in the Commander in Chief's lap powers to determine civilian concerns. Although he fought off rather than sought these extensions of responsibility and made as little use of them as was feasible, Washington became, while still Commander in Chief, as much of a chief executive as the United States then had.

This did not escape observation, and many influential patriots considered that the possibility of making Washington a one-man government was an asset which could be fallen back on in a severe emergency. As we have seen, he had been begged by major political leaders to take over the government of Virginia. In May, 1782, he had received from one of his colonels, Lewis Nicola, a letter urging him to accept the responsibility of becoming king of the United States.

The suggestion seemed to Nicola highly reasonable. Every major nation in the world was then ruled by a king, and royalty had been throughout history almost exclusively the accepted form of government. But Washington replied, "No occurrence in the course of the war has given me more painful sensations than your information of there being such ideas existing in the army. . . . I must view with abhorrence and reprehend with severity" a conception that was "big with the greatest mischiefs that can befall my country."

However, Washington had taken this stand before it was known that the states would not of their own volition make possible a central government strong enough even to pay its just debts to the national creditors and to the soldiers who had fought under his leadership for so many years.

Washington was at his headquarters on the banks of the Hudson at Newburgh, New York, when, during mid-February of 1783, Hamilton's effort to inveigle him arrived in the form of a subtly composed letter. As a congressman, Hamilton reported that there were no further possibilities of supplying the army; by June, the troops would have to take everything they needed at bayonet point. As a colonel (he was still a member of the army), Hamilton informed Washington that, should peace come, the army intended to use its bayonets "to procure justice to itself."

Washington's own command, so Hamilton warned, was in danger. The army felt that his "delicacy carried to an extreme" had made him stand in the way of their achieving their just dues. They might very well act without him. Then "the difficulty will be to keep a complaining and suffering army within the bounds of moderation." But if Washington took the lead, the result could be salutary rather than destructive. By cooperating with "all men of sense," the army could, under Washington's benign control, operate on "weak minds" to establish the federal taxation "which alone can do justice to the creditors of the United States . . . and supply the future wants of government."

In came a letter from one of Washington's confidential correspondents, Congressman Joseph Jones of Virginia. Jones warned that "dangerous combinations in the army" were using "sinister practices" to tear down Washington's reputation so that "the weight of your opposition will prove no obstacle to their ambitious designs." Jones believed that the plot was likely to succeed. "Whether to temporize or oppose with steady, unremitting firmness," he continued, " . . . must be left to your own sense of propriety and better judgement."

During "many contemplative hours," Washington, as he put it, puzzled over "the predicament in which I stand as a citizen and soldier." In that year of 1783, the efforts of the United States to establish a republican government were unique in the world. Modern history presented no evidence that people could rule themselves. Even political philosophers who thought that the people might under some circumstances be able to do so, commonly believed that republican forms could only survive on a small scale — and was this not being demonstrated by the behavior of the states? Even worse: it was generally believed in Europe that efforts at popular rule could only eventuate in anarchy and chaos. As Washington paced in perplexity, anarchy and chaos seemed about to overwhelm America. Was it not his patriotic duty, as Hamilton said, to accept the inevitable, as he had so often done on physical battlefields? And what of his ambitions? In a world of kings, why should not George Washington also be a king? He was later to thank the Ruler of the Universe — "the Greatest and Best of Beings" — for having led him "to detest the folly and madness of unbounded ambition."

Yet, when he placed ambition behind him, that only made the situation more "difficult and delicate." The injustices being visited on the army were obvious and no peaceful remedies were in sight. His own investigations revealed that the army was more rebellious than he had realized, and that his leadership was in fact under severe attack. He suspected his old enemy General Gates, who was finally back in active service, of being deep in the intrigue.

It was early March before Washington answered Hamilton's letter. He could not, he wrote, countenance a movement which would be "productive of civil commotions and end in blood." Despite the menace to his own leadership and reputation, "I shall pursue the same steady line of conduct which has governed me hitherto; fully convinced that the sensible and discerning part of the army cannot be unacquainted (although I never took pains to inform them) of the services I have rendered it on more occasions than one."

Washington's letter made it clear that the conspirators would have to proceed independently, either catching him up in the tempest they raised or blowing him aside.

Through the camp at Newburgh, unsigned papers began circulating. One ignored Washington's authority by calling a mass meeting of officers. Another stated that the author had lost faith "in the justice of his country." He urged his fellow soldiers to "suspect the man who would advise to more moderation and further forbearance." If peace should be declared, nothing should separate the army "from your arms but death." If the war continued, "courting the auspices and inviting the direction of your illustrious leader, you will retire to some unsettled country, smile in your turn, and 'mock when their fear cometh on.'"

Washington was himself deeply moved by the anonymous author's emotional description of the soldier's plight — he felt that the "force of expression has rarely been equaled in the English language" — but he believed it his duty "to arrest on the spot the foot that stood wavering on a tremendous precipice, to prevent the officers from being taken by surprise while the passions were all inflamed, and to rescue them from plunging themselves into a gulf of civil horror from which there might be no receding."

The Commander in Chief expressed "disapprobation of such disorderly proceedings" as the illegally called meeting. He summoned a meeting of his own for the following Saturday, March 15, 1783. This was probably the most important single gathering ever held in the United States. Supposing, as seemed only too possible, Washington should fail to prevent military intervention in civil government?

The Commander in Chief hinted that he would not appear personally, and thus when he strode on the stage, it was a surprise. And the faces of his gathered officers made it clear that the surprise was not a pleasant one. For the first time since he had won the love of the army, he saw facing him resentment and anger.

As Washington began to speak, he was "sensibly agitated." He talked first of his own early and devoted service, of his love for his soldiers. The faces before him did not soften. He pointed out that the country which the anonymous exhorter wished them to tyrannize over or abandon was their own: "our wives, our children, our farms and other property." As for the exhorter's advice that they should refuse to listen to words of moderation, this would mean that "reason is of no use to us. The freedom of speech may be taken away, and, dumb and silent, we may be led, like sheep, to the slaughter." By now, the audience seemed perturbed, but the anger and resentment had not been dispelled.

Washington then stated that he believed the government would, "despite the slowness inherent in deliberative bodies," in the end act justly. He urged the officers not "to open the flood gates of civil discord, and deluge our rising empire in blood." They should "afford occasion for posterity to say, when speaking of the glorious example you have exhibited to mankind, 'had this day been wanting, the world had never seen the last stage of perfection to which human nature is capable of attaining.'"

Washington had come to the end of his prepared speech but his audience did not seem truly moved. He clearly had not achieved his end. He remembered he had brought with him a reassuring letter from a congressman. He would read it. He pulled the paper from his pocket, and then something seemed to go wrong. The General seemed confused; he stared at the paper helplessly. The officers leaned forward, their hearts contracting with anxiety. Washington pulled from his pocket something only his intimates had seen him wear: a pair of eyeglasses. "Gentlemen," he said, "you will permit me to put on my spectacles, for I have not only grown gray but almost blind in the service of my country."

This homely act and simple statement did what all Washington's arguments had failed to do. The hardened soldiers wept. Washington had saved the United States from tyranny and civil discord. As Jefferson was later to comment, "The moderation and virtue of a single character probably prevented this Revolution from being closed, as most others have been, by a subversion of that liberty it was intended to establish."

On April 18, 1783, Washington's general orders announced "the cessation of hostilities between the United States of America and the King of Great Britain." Although the peace treaty had not been signed, the armistice, so Washington continued, "opens the prospect to a more splendid scene, and, like another morning star, promises the approach of a brighter day than hath hitherto illuminated the western hemisphere." He congratulated the troops on "the dignified part they have been called to act (under the smiles of Providence) on the stage of human affairs; for happy, thrice happy, shall they be pronounced hereafter who have contributed anything, who have performed the meanest office in erecting this stupendous fabric of Freedom and Empire on the broad basis of Independency; who have assisted in protecting the rights of human nature and established an asylum for the poor and oppressed of all nations and religions."

Although Washington's praises comprised civilians as well as soldiers, he did not feel warmly towards the financiers who had, as he came increasingly to realize, played a major part in the efforts to induce the army to dictate to the civilian governments. He wrote Hamilton, angrily, "The army . . . is a dangerous instrument to play with." In his appeals to Congress, and through Congress to the nation, that what was owed to the army should be paid, he made no reference to the debts owed the financiers. But concerning his fellow soldiers he was emotional. If they were forced "to wade through the vile mire of despondency and owe 'the miserable remnant of that life to charity which has hitherto been spent in honor,' then I shall have learned what ingratitude is; then I shall have realized a tale which will embitter every moment of my future life."

As lesser verbal artillery gave no indication of ameliorating the situation, Washington decided to send to the states a circular letter which would dig deep into the political fundamentals of the problem. He justified thus stepping out of his military role, and also endowed his words with a special solemnity, by announcing that this was his farewell to public life. Once the final peace permitted him to return to Mount Vernon, he would never again "take any share in public business."

Privately, Washington was already urging such a constitutional convention as would not be convened until five years and much history had passed by. He yearned for a new "federal constitution" which would cut the power of the states down to dealing with primarily local problems. But he realized that this was too radical a suggestion to be included in the circular letter that came to be known as "Washington's Legacy." In this document, he only urged that the Articles of Confederation be interpreted and extended to create a central government adequate to obvious needs. Unless this were achieved, the Americans might "find by our own unhappy experience that there is a natural and necessary progression from the extreme of anarchy to the extreme of tyranny."

Until the armistice was followed by a final treaty, peace was not official. However, Congress decided to send home all of the army except a small force to watch the British troops who were awaiting in New York the final peace. Congress passed resolutions directed at keeping the released soldiers from departing penniless, but resolutions buy nothing and there was no money available. As they prepared to depart with empty pockets, the officers expressed great bitterness at having allowed themselves to be bamboozled by Washington: they canceled a farewell dinner at which he was to be guest of honor. "The sensibility," Washington wrote, "occasioned by a parting scene under such peculiar circumstances will not admit of description."

Despite his yearning to get back to Mount Vernon, Washington decided that his duty would not permit him to abandon the remnant of his army who remained encamped on the Hudson. He had to "wear away," as he wrote, seven months of "this distressing tedium." Some relaxation was supplied by a trip around the northern frontier, where he examined the sites of battles he had not commanded; and a period of attending on Congress, during which he made recommendations for a peacetime military establishment which that powerless legislature was too debilitated to enact.

After the definitive peace had been signed, the British announced that they would evacuate New York on November 25, 1783. For once, Washington was willing to take part in a triumphal procession. However, the parade was ridiculously delayed because the British had, in a final mocking gesture, left their flag flying over Fort George with the halyards cut and the pole greased. Not until an ingenious sailor had mounted the pole and substituted an American flag could Washington consummate victory by advancing down the streets. It was as sad an occasion as a joyful one, for the city was desolate and battered, the few inhabitants who came out to cheer were thin and strained. There was a further wait until the British fleet finally sailed out of the harbor. Then Washington ordered a boat to take him across the Hudson to New Jersey. But first he would say farewell to the few officers still in service and to any others residing in the vicinity.

The assurances Washington had given his officers, during that stormy meeting at Newburgh, that they would receive what was due them had, despite his own best efforts, come to nothing. He approached this last parting with a sad and anxious heart. The small group of men who turned as he came in the door of the room at Fraunces Tavern saw that their general's face was working with strong emotion. He walked over to the table where a collation was laid, tried to eat, but failed. He filled a glass of wine and motioned for the decanters to go around. As the officers saw his hand shake and his lip tremble, the bitterness in their hearts was drowned by love. The men who had fought so hard with Washington and suffered so deeply found tears in their eyes. With tears streaming down his own face, Washington embraced each separately, and then, the height of emotion having become unbearable, walked out of the room.

Washington left New York on December 4. His trip to Annapolis, where Congress was meeting, was clogged by crowds who wished to do him honor. The ceremony before Congress during which he returned his commission, was again wet with tears. Then, after almost nine years of service, he was free. As he rode up the circular drive to Mount Vernon, there were candles in the windows. Martha stood in the doorway. It was Christmas Eve.

Debates have raged concerning Washington's ability as a soldier. Writers have contended that he was so incompetent that he would have been defeated by any other human beings except the dullards the British sent against him. He has been described as an equal of Caesar, Hannibal, Napoleon. The debate has overlooked the fact that Washington was never really a soldier. He was a civilian in arms.

Civilians had always seemed more important to him than soldiers. However, since there was a war, an army was an essential instrument. It should guard and preserve the population to the greatest extent it could. To repel that civilian discouragement which could foster a wavering of loyalty to the cause, the soldiers should seek an impressive record. (Washington often helped the record along with inaccurate dispatches.) Washington further realized that a war won primarily by the force of public opinion would of necessity be a war of attrition, a very long war. He yearned for military victories that would cut the process short. But he knew that victories involving brutality against civilians and thus achieved at the expense of public opinion, would, in fact, be defeats.

Washington's belief that the war was more basically a civilian than a military conflict was underlined by chronology. From his assumption of the command to the last battle he led against the main British army was almost exactly three years. From the Battle of Monmouth to the final departure of the British army was four and a half. The second period contained, of course, the largely French-engineered victory at Yorktown. Yet Cornwallis's surrender was not in essence a much more serious defeat than Burgoyne's, and the conditions that had made it possible evaporated with the departure of the French fleet so completely that there was no reason for the British to believe that this enemy triumph could ever be repeated. They would have regarded Yorktown as no more than an unfortunate check were they not being gravely defeated on more important battlefields. They came to realize the utter hopelessness of conquering a people who had become united against them. Washington's role in fostering this unity had been great.

Washington entered the contest almost as entirely untrained in sophisticated warfare as were his troops. The British and Hessians were very well trained. Until Washington got over fighting European regulars in the conventional manner, the Continental Army went down to defeat after defeat. The break came with Trenton and Princeton, when Washington made use of the particular qualities of dedicated soldiers who would march quickly in the face of any hardship; would fight with brilliance individually if not so well in formation; and exist on nonexistent supplies. These qualities were particularly suited to American economic and political disorganization, which made the loss of even the national capital not crippling and to the American terrain, which encouraged guerrilla warfare and made formal battles easy to avoid.

Being practically without schooling, Washington had always taught himself from experience. He learned the lessons of the American war all the more readily because he had no conventional lessons to unlearn. The British and the Hessians, on the other hand, suffered the confusion common to acknowledged experts when their expertise ceases to function. Instead of seeking new solutions, they felt they were up against something inexplicable and became increasingly timid. Back in London, another foreseeable reaction took place: If an expert does not deliver as he should, you replace him with another who is expected to apply the accepted rules more effectively. Washington survived four British commanders in chief.

Long before the end of the war, Washington had become much more effective than any of his military opponents. But this did not mean that what he had taught himself would have made him a great general on the battlefields of Europe. Evolved not from theory but from dealing with specific problems, his preeminence was achieved through a Darwinian adaptation to environment. It was the triumph of a man who knows how to learn, not in the narrow sense of studying other people's conceptions, but in the transcendent sense of making a synthesis from the totality of experience.

Among the legacies of the Revolution to the new nation, the most widely recognized and admired was a man: George Washington. He had no rivals. When the war ended, not a single officer was really powerful in the army who had not been elevated and trained by the Commander in Chief—and who was not loyal to him. In the civilian sphere no individual had national stature comparable with Washington's. The General had more than any political figure served as the nation's chief executive. Yet no continuation of leadership figured in his happy imaginings.

"At length, my dear Marquis," Washington wrote Lafayette, "I am become a private citizen on the banks of the Potomac, and under the shadow of my own vine and my own fig tree. Free from the bustle of a camp and the busy scenes of public life, I am solacing myself with those tranquil enjoyments which the soldier who is ever in pursuit of fame; the statesman whose watchful days and sleepless nights are spent in devising schemes to promote the welfare of his own, perhaps the ruin of other countries (as if this globe was insufficient for all); and the courtier who is always watching the countenance of his prince, in hopes of catching a gracious smile, can have very little conception. I am not only retired from all public employments, but I am retiring within myself, and shall be able to view the solitary walk and tread the paths of private life with heartfelt satisfaction. Envious of none, I am determined to be pleased with all, and this, my dear friend, being the order of my march, I will move gently down the stream of life until I sleep with my fathers."

Questions for Discussion

1. Given that revolutions prior to the American Revolution most often ended in tyranny, what made the outcome different in this case? Would there have been a United States without George Washington? What characteristics do you see in him that inspired his men to endure further hardship rather than attempt to alleviate their suffering by taking over the political system?

2. Washington was, as Flexner notes, every bit as much a chief executive for the United States during the Revolution as he was its military commander. How do you explain his rejection of the idea that he ought to become a king? If Washington had agreed to lead or take part in a military coup, what do you think would have happened to the idea of civilian control over the military?

3. The mechanisms of our Republic often are, by design, slow and deliberative. How do you explain the system's enduring success in light of its incremental approach to even the most pressing problems? What strengths of republican government compensate for its gradualism?

6 John Quincy Adams:
A Public Life,
A Private Life

PAUL C. NAGEL

After serving as president, John Quincy Adams was later elected to the U.S. House. It was there that he made a great contribution to the nation by fighting the 1836 'gag rule' — a parliamentary procedure that allowed the House of Representatives to table any petition or debate on any issue, especially, at that time, slavery. As with others, Quincy Adams's moral outrage against the South's "slavocracy" evolved gradually, but his overriding principles led him to oppose the restrictive 'gag rule.' The more he opposed it, the more the lines were drawn between Adams's focus on universal human rights and southern congressmen's preservation of slavery. A great battle of oratory and political maneuvering ensued.

ACTUALLY, THE LIGHT he had craved led John Quincy Adams toward not one but two causes. Both would benefit the American republic, as well as humanity at large. The first was a defense of the right of petition. The other was to create a federal institution devoted to scholarship. These stands were often so unpopular in Congress that Adams had the pleasure of thinking he stood alone against all the malevolence in the universe.

The fight that brought luster to Adams's congressional career began during the winter of 1836. While his eventual aim was to corral slavery, at first he struggled only in behalf of a citizen's right to petition the government. The right prevailed, he said, even if a petitioner should be addressing slavery, a subject taboo to many Americans. His argument drew fierce opposition from the southern slavocracy and the northern followers of Andrew Jackson. The result made him the most famous — or notorious — combatant on the floor of Congress during the next decade.

Ironically, Adams's seemingly brilliant decision to make the right of petition his cause involved mostly luck. While his defense of petitioners soon earned him worldwide repute as a bitter enemy of slavery, he had not selected the issue because of its link to human bondage. Previously he had displayed little concern about the enslaved African-American. Shortly after leaving the White House, he assured his diary that there was "misapprehension and much prejudice" about the treatment of bondsmen; perhaps a few cases of "extreme oppression and cruelty" did exist on southern plantations, he conceded, but "I believe them to be very rare, and that the general treatment of slaves is mild and moderate."

By 1836, however, he recognized that bondage appeared likely to be a permanent painful presence in the republic. What vexed him about this development was less that human beings were being degraded than that the nation must listen to southern politicians spout a "torrent of moral depravity" in justifying slavery. Adams remembered, of course, that many of these southerners had smeared his name and helped defeat him in 1828. In short, the Southern politicos had been and remained scoundrels as far as he was concerned.

He believed that owning slaves was only one of the sins committed by this group, among whom he saw a general depravity in behavior that produced men like Jefferson, Jackson, Crawford, Calhoun, and others whom Adams scorned or despised. Consequently, when he began militantly to oppose the South, it was mainly because he believed the region's representatives were unprincipled, and thus a threat to the health of the country.

While he ultimately enlisted in the crusade against slavery, Adams never supported the abolitionists. Indeed, for a time some of them were among his bitter critics after he announced that Congress had no power to emancipate slaves in the District of Columbia. He charged that radicals such as William Lloyd Garrison would willingly dissolve the Union to satisfy their ends, and disunion, he argued, would be a disaster for civilization's experiment with democracy. To avert such a catastrophe, he was content to tolerate slavery where it existed while insisting that the nation must guarantee the right of petition, even for petitions that urged slavery's abolition.

Consequently, Adams was outraged when, after sharp debate, the House of Representatives adopted a new parliamentary procedure in May 1836 that became known as the gag rule. He had done what he could to oppose approving the rule, which decreed that all petitions or memorials touching in any way on slavery would be laid on the table without being printed, discussed, or referred to committee. Southern congressmen had demanded the rule after the anti-slavery movement began flooding Congress with petitions calling particularly for the ending of slavery and the slave trade in the District of Columbia. Adams had found his mail bulging with them.

He had made a sensation of himself during the House discussion over adopting the gag rule. His search for just the right cause was ended as he began to deride and denounce the enemies of petition. While his voice might be shrilled by age and his language often extreme and outrageous, he now felt justified in using every mental and emotional strength — and weakness — in fighting to have petitions properly received by the House.

In doing so, he rejoiced that he could oppose those persons, particularly the Jackson Democrats of the North, who believed with Martin Van Buren that being silent about slavery was a small price to pay for party unity and electoral victory. By accepting the gag rule, these Yankees gave Adams a hefty weapon with which to avenge himself against many longtime adversaries. He argued impressively that a citizen's right to have a petition received and heard was so essential for free government that it took on religious sanctity.

As the kind of cause Adams had prayed for, opposing the gag rule allowed him to defend high principle while at the same time exposing his opponents as evildoers. His assault on the slaveholders' congressional bloc soon became a lively topic in America's public discourse. What drew attention was the emergence of a new John Quincy Adams. His adopted cause transformed him into a debater so impassioned, so mischievous, so stubborn, and so radical that his foes and even some friends wondered at times if he had lost his sanity.

While others might try to cheer him on or shout him down, his wife and son watched this new Adams with a mingling of sorrow and sympathy. After forty years of marriage, Louisa could appreciate what motivated her spouse. Among her journal jottings during the congressional uproar in 1836 was an expression of hope that his aspiration would be realized — "that he may leave a fame to posterity and awaken the justice of this nation to record his name as one of the fairest midst the race of man." Adams himself could not have stated his yearning more succinctly.

At other moments, however, Louisa fretted at the personal cost her husband was beginning to pay as a zealot in Congress. "Could he only bring his mind to the calm of retirement," she wrote, knowing that it meant he must put aside "mortified vanity" and "disappointed ambition." But invariably, she was compelled to admit that if he did step down, it would destroy him. The situation left Louisa with a revealing regret: yielding to no one in her admiration for her husband's strengths, she believed that by fighting in Congress, he was wasting "all the energies of his fine mind upon a people who do not either understand or appreciate his talents."

Charles Francis Adams, an astute observer of his father, took a more down-to-earth view. "My own opinion is and has been for many years that his whole system of life is very wrong—that he sleeps by far too little, that he eats and drinks too irregularly, and that he has habituated his mind to a state of morbid activity which makes life in its common forms very tedious." Yet to try calming his father was hopeless, Charles conceded. Even when the admired Boston physician Dr. Jacob Bigelow gave JQA written instructions to seek a quiet existence, the aging warrior disregarded the advice. . . .

With the heroic in mind, Adams finally was able to limp back to the House in time to enter the heated debate over whether the new slaveholding Republic of Texas should join the Union. He stoutly opposed the idea, but found it difficult to gain the floor. Repeatedly, but with rare success, he sought to speak or vote amid the shouts against him by defenders of slavery, who demanded "order, order." In reply, he taunted them by yelling, "Am I gagged, am I gagged?" The acrimony became so bitter that he confided to his diary: "I shall henceforth speak in the House of Representatives at the hazard of my life." . . .

The floor of the House was not always the scene of titanic conflict. Perhaps more typical was the day when Adams privately complained that much less than a quorum was present, "and of them about half were slumbering in their seats, and the other half yawning over newspapers." A very few walked about "to keep up the circulation of the blood," while each "settee" held a distinguished member "stretched out [and] sound asleep." What Adams preferred to describe were the days when pandemonium ruled as members, mostly from the South, tried to subdue the person whom some of them called "the Madman from Massachusetts."

He could be fiendishly clever in presenting petitions from abolitionists and from Peace Society members. Although it was slow going, Adams's strategy began to succeed. He encouraged his northern colleagues to insist that petitions from citizens who were against Texas' entering the Union should be received, even if they bore on the unmentionable issue of Negro bondage. Once northern Democrats were enticed from their southern colleagues by this issue, Adams foresaw that there would soon be votes sufficient to overturn the gag rule.

His parliamentary tactics were unmatched by any House colleague. On June 16, 1838, through skillful maneuvering, he was able to have the floor for his own purposes during the "morning hour" before topics scheduled for the day were called up. He used the time for a speech that consumed parts of fifteen days. His subject was "Freedom of Speech," a topic broad enough to allow him to flay the slaveowners. Claiming that slavery was "a sin before the sight of God," he asserted that to bring Texas into the Union would only enlarge the evil. . . .

Before Congress resumed on December 3, Adams thought he sensed a growing friendliness toward him in the capital. When he made a perfunctory call at the White House, President Van Buren carefully reassured him that the Smithson bequest would be used honorably. Then came an invitation to dine at the home of Treasury Secretary Levi Woodbury. Upon arriving, Adams discovered that the other guests included the president and members of the cabinet, as well as an assortment of foreign ministers. Mrs. Woodbury and her daughter being the only women present, JQA was asked to escort Miss Woodbury to the table while Van Buren took in the lady of the house. The meal then proceeded, with Adams and the president seated at the places of honor beside their hostess. JQA noted with satisfaction that most other guests "might have disputed my seat, with me a simple member of the House, but no pretensions were made."

When the House began business, there were also touches of civility displayed toward him by many of the 210 members. "Mutual greetings," Adams sourly noted, adding, "cordial on the lips." True enough. It was the calm before a storm that lasted through the three months of the session. Much of the tumult was caused by JQA, whose aggressiveness had not been softened by any courtesies shown him in Washington or Boston. But no matter how he fought, the gag rule was reimposed.

During the battle, however, a further change had come over the member from Quincy as he sat amid the "yells" and "agonized lungs" of his Southern opponents. Although he spoke of how he "dissected and pulverized" the arguments of his enemies, Adams now seemed bored and impatient with the petition battle. With relief, he accepted an invitation from the New-York Historical Society to deliver the principal address when on April 30, 1839, the society celebrated the fiftieth anniversary of George Washington's inauguration as president.

Pleased though he was by the task, he made little progress until Congress adjourned on March 4, and then he had to pause for his usual misgivings: "The subject is rugged with insurmountable difficulties. My reputation, my age, my decaying faculties, have all warned me to decline the task." To do justice to the celebrated day "would require a younger hand and a brighter mind." But having said this, he proceeded to write three pages a day, all the time wondering why the assignment worried him. "Such is my nature, and I shall have no quiet of mind till it is over."

Once again, he fretted needlessly. The great moment arrived, and Adams found himself surrounded by admiring New Yorkers. He admitted that the oration, which lasted two hours, was "well received" before a packed house. Afterward he was the honored guest at a dinner where three hundred persons assembled.

The speech, which proved to be one of Adams's best, emphasized that America's historic moment of greatness came with the decision at the Constitutional Convention to put aside "the irresponsible despotism of state sovereignty" and create a Union based on the self-evident truths espoused by the Declaration of Independence. In this manner, he introduced the inflammatory issue of universal human rights, which he had been extolling in Congress. By creating a Union pledged to uphold human dignity, he said, the American people had "achieved the most transcendent act of power that social man in his mental condition can perform." Such a Union, he contended, was indissoluble, since it rested "not in the sight, but in the heart." It lifted the word "*Union!*" into what he called "the simultaneous cry throughout the land." Thus did he warn the South that the federal Union was no casual agreement to be easily put aside.

The oration was immediately published as "Jubilee of the Constitution." In a few weeks, eight thousand copies had been sold by the society, and demand was rising. It was an unprecedented success, the New Yorkers assured Adams, who had himself done much to spread the fame of his remarks. Among JQA's surviving papers are carefully prepared pages of names of the individuals, famous and unsung, to whom he presented a personal copy of the speech. Not even his nieces and nephews were overlooked.

Thrilled by this enthusiasm, Adams said that "in this dark and declining stage of my existence," the address marked an accomplishment for which he "could never be sufficiently grateful to God." To dampen any excessive delight, he predicted that it would receive a few "puffs" of attention and then "it is forgotten." He was quite wrong. The public's favorable response made "Jubilee of the Constitution" one of the most influential statements concerning the nature of the federal Union. It would continue to be quoted on the eve of the Civil War and afterward. . . .

From the start of 1841, Adams used every available moment to prepare for his first appearance before the United States Supreme Court since 1809. At the urging of Lewis Tappan, one of the founders of the American Anti-Slavery Society and a world leader in the movement, and other leading opponents of human bondage, he had agreed to join the distinguished attorney Roger S. Baldwin as counsel in defending thirty-nine Africans, whose story, along with John Quincy Adams's part in it, became a powerful weapon for the anti-slavery cause in America.

The Africans had been captives on the Spanish slave ship *Amistad* until they seized the vessel as it was sailing along the coast of Cuba in July 1839. The whites on board, however, gave the mutineers misleading navigational advice, which led the ship not back to Africa, as the blacks wished, but toward Long Island, New York. There the U.S. Navy discovered the vessel in late August. The Africans were taken to New Haven, Connecticut, where they were lodged in jail while their fate became an international issue.

In 1840, federal judges at both district and circuit levels had no difficulty deciding that the *Amistad* prisoners were not property but human beings, unlawfully seized in Africa and hauled off by their captors to be sold into Cuban slavery. What brought Adams into the controversy was his indignation over the appeal of these lower-court decisions to the Supreme Court by the Van Buren administration, whose lofty talk of treaty rights and the law of the seas masked its reluctance to free the captives and thereby anger southerners in an election year. The Supreme Court case was scheduled to open on February 22, 1841.

Some days before the hearing, a very nervous Adams made a serious mistake. He became so anxious over his role in the case that he lost control of his temper in the House and created what was, even for him, a mortifying scene. It arose out of his outrage at the domineering style of Congressman Henry A. Wise of Virginia, whose parliamentary maneuvers brought Adams to make an hour's speech in which, as he himself described the episode, he "arraigned . . . before the world the principles avowed by Henry A. Wise, and his three-colored standard, of overseer, black, dueling, blood-red, and dirty, cadaverous nullification white."

Afterward, Adams was appalled by his extreme language, even if it was aimed at a despised southerner. He feared that his allies might well think him the victim of an "eccentric, wild, extravagant" fit of "passion." And indeed, *insane* was an adjective some House members applied to him, leaving him yearning for "firmness to rule my own spirit." A still-shaken Adams carried the distressing memory of the Wise encounter into the Supreme Court's presence.

In the Court's room beneath the Senate chamber, he heard Roger Baldwin make the defense's opening arguments in the *Amistad* case. A day later, with fears that he would be a miserable failure, Adams rose to present the closing statement. Faltering at first, he was soon strengthened by confidence in his cause and by the presence of a large audience. His voice held out, and his thoughts became more orderly in an argument described by Justice Joseph Story as an astonishing blend of power, "bitter sarcasm," and topics "far beyond the record and points of discussion."

By this, Story was referring mostly to Adams's detours to denounce the Van Buren administration's effort to whisk the blacks out of the country and back to slavery. JQA also gave much time to exulting in the highest moral and judicial precepts, with the result that, even after speaking beyond four hours, he had not finished when the Court adjourned.

Later that day, Justice Philip Barbour died, so that readings did not resume until March 1, when a rested Adams took another four hours to complete his remarks. For him, the *Amistad* case was quite simple. Uniting with the abolitionists and less radical opponents of slavery, he pushed aside maritime law and property rights in order to exalt human liberty under natural law. It was much the same position taken by the lower courts.

Concluding with one of his most eloquent public statements, Adams talked of the noble service rendered by many justices now deceased — which led him to pray that each jurist sitting before him might go "to his final account with as little of earthly frailty to answer for as those illustrious dead." The judges on the bench may well have wondered whether the former president was issuing a gentle warning in expressing the hope that they might someday enter the heavenly gates to hear, "Well done, thou good and faithful servant."

Five days later the majority decision, in which Chief Justice Roger Taney concurred, was read by Justice Story. With only one dissent, the Court found for Adams's side. The Africans were declared free men, and eventually they returned to their homeland. JQA's performance in their behalf lifted him even higher in the esteem of the American public north of the Mason-Dixon Line. The praise led him to concede that, "although I fell immeasurably short of my wishes in that case, I did not utterly disappoint the public expectation."

Encouraged by his *Amistad* triumph, as well as by the inauguration of Harrison as president on March 4, Adams paid no heed to suggestions that he retire from office amid the glow of personal and party victory. On the contrary, he was eager to remain in Washington. And, indeed, why not? The president informed all within earshot that he considered Adams an old friend, indeed almost a brother. At White House dinners, Harrison customarily slapped him on the back and invited him to make the first toast.

But the sweetest moment came when Harrison asserted that Adams was the chief executive who "had been so unjustly put out." Afterward, a glowing JQA admitted that redeeming his name had been costly, for politics was now for him "as much a necessary of life as atmospheric air." Calling this addiction a weakness he could not control, he predicted that "the world will retire from me before I shall retire from the world." . . .

When the House convened, he had the satisfaction of being named chairman of two committees concerned with his pet interests: foreign relations and the Smithson bequest. If his colleagues anticipated that this tribute would divert Congressman Adams from making a commotion over the gag rule or from seizing any opportunity to attack slavery, they were badly mistaken. By the close of January, a movement was under way in the House to censure him. Led by southerners, the effort was nothing less, Adams claimed, than "a conspiracy in and out of Congress to crush the liberties of the free people of the Union." The exhilaration of battle led him to elevate the struggle to sublime heights when he asserted that the slavocracy, which meant about one hundred members of the House, "would crucify me if their vote could erect the cross."

The furor erupted on January 21, 1842, during Adams's annual campaign to restore free speech by repealing the gag rule. This time his strategy was to present a petition from citizens of Georgia urging that he be removed as chairman of the Foreign Relations Committee — which obliged the House to allow him to retain the floor on a point of personal privilege. Under the circumstances, a speaker would use the time to defend himself, but instead of doing so Adams flayed the "Southern slave traders" for seeking to get him out of the way of their plot to bring slaveholding Texas into the Union.

The indignation of southern members at Adams's stratagem astonished even seasoned onlookers in the House gallery. A typical shout to the Speaker was "I demand that you shut the mouth of that old harlequin." Undismayed, Adams brought forward an even more electrifying petition. From citizens of Haverhill, Massachusetts, the plea urged Congress to dissolve the Union, claiming that because so much federal money was spent supporting southern institutions, the Union had become an unrewarding burden on free states. Although he slyly said that the time was not yet at hand for disunion, his adversaries insisted that, at last, he had gone too far by introducing such an inflammatory idea.

At first, the anti-Adams spokesmen proposed merely that he be reprimanded for mentioning the subject of disunion. But after a Kentuckian offered a resolution that accused him of "the crime of high treason," most southern representatives succumbed to blind anger and agreed to try to censure Adams, claiming that he had "disgraced his country" and merited the "severest" punishment. But the resolution of censure proved to be a fatal mistake. Adams immediately claimed the right, which belonged to any citizen, of defending himself against charges of treason. Thus, the debate over censure became a judicial proceeding, wherein the masterly JQA converted his defense into an offense. It allowed him to describe his situation with a grand flourish: he faced, he said, "a trial [in] which the liberties of my country are enduring in my person."

When moderate southerners and their northern allies saw the tactical mistake made by hotheaded colleagues, they tried to shelve the attempt to censure. But Adams arranged for the motion to table the resolution to be defeated so that he might continue what seemed an interminable scourging of southerners, whom he pictured as befoulers of the nation's sacred freedoms. As a result, it soon was no longer Adams but southerners who stood trial. As his "defense" stretched across two weeks, he took time to make personal indictments of individuals he despised. He shouted that one member who was recently in a duel had "his hands and face dripping with the blood of murder."

Throughout his "trial," Adams was in his glory. He knew that the resolution indicting him would probably fail, and if it passed, he would resign, convinced that his constituents would immediately vote to return him to his seat. While he recognized that his struggle against "persecution" had earned him cheers from the free states, his main delight was in knowing that southerners would forever see him as "the acutest, the astutest, the archest enemy of Southern slavery that ever existed," in the words of Virginia's Henry A. Wise.

Eventually, even Adams saw that the fracas ought to end and allowed the censure motion to come to a vote. It was defeated 106 to 93 on February 4. Most opponents of slavery claimed Adams's acquittal as their first victory over the South, bringing hope that soon the slavocracy would no longer rule the government of the United States. . . .

. . . [O]n December 3, he had reason to utter a fervent prayer of thanks to the Lord of the Sabbath. "Blessed, forever blessed, be the name of God!" he intoned, for the victory he had prayed for was won. By 108 to 80, a gratifying margin, the House had voted to approve Adams's resolution rescinding the hated gag rule. Thereafter, petitioners who urged the abolition of slavery and the slave trade would be freely heard. . . .

Questions for Discussion

1.   Critical of the most militant abolitionists, John Quincy Adams became a harsh critic of slavery. How did he ultimately turn his criticism of the congressional 'gag rule' into a trial of his opponents and their values, rather than himself?

2.   What were Adams's weaknesses, and how did they needlessly provide ammunition for his political foes? Would you have advised him to take a less tempestuous approach to his causes, or was it better that he remained true to his convictions in a fiery way?

3.   Adams provides a telling example of the influence that a former president — even one who may be perceived at the end of his time in office as having done a mediocre job — can exert on the nation. Should ex-presidents play high-profile leadership roles in national politics, or should they exit the stage?

7 With Malice Toward None: The Life of Abraham Lincoln

STEPHEN OATES

In this essay, historian Stephen Oates explores several dimensions of Abraham Lincoln — politician, storyteller, and reader of Shakespeare's tragedies. What most consumed Lincoln, though, was his role as Commander in Chief. The demands of leading a nation in peacetime are enormous. But during wartime? During a civil war? As Lincoln dealt with the myriad details of mobilizing the nation for war and with the harsh criticisms of many of his presidential decisions, Lincoln as leader found direction in his singular moral quest — preserving the Union.

IF LINCOLN WAS GOING to suppress "this giant insurrection," he must have capable generals as well as a trained army, but there lay the problem. At the time Sumter fell, the small regular army was a shambles, depleted by Southern resignations and run by senior officers like Scott who were too old and infirm to lead a field command. Only Scott and muttering old John Wool had ever led armies, the largest of which had been the fourteen-thousand-man expeditionary force Scott had taken into Mexico back in 1847. None of the junior officers had even directed the evolution of a brigade.

Scott himself admitted that a younger officer should take field command of the army. When Lincoln's call for troops went out, Scott recommended Colonel Robert E. Lee of the First Cavalry, whose family mansion could be seen up on Arlington Heights south of the Potomac. Lee had graduated from West Point, fought in the Mexican War, served on the Texas border, and captured John Brown at Harpers Ferry a year and a half ago. The colonel was married to Martha Custis — daughter of George Washington's adopted son — and had an awesome reverence for the first President, whom Lee strove to emulate. Lincoln liked Scott's suggestion and authorized Frank Blair, Sr., to invite the colonel into Washington for a talk. On April 18, the day after the Virginia convention voted for secession, Blair met with Lee in his Washington home and unofficially offered Lee field command of the Union army, insisting that he spoke for the President. But Lee declined the offer. He conceded that he opposed secession, considered it "anarchy, nothing but revolution," and that he abhorred civil war as well. Though he didn't say so now, Lee also regarded slavery as a "moral and political evil" — yet he enjoyed the grace and status of plantation life and showed no willingness to emancipate the two hundred or so slaves he managed on his Virginia estate. No matter how he felt about the slave system, he detested Northern abolitionists, often vented his temper on "those fanatics," and blamed them for the present crisis. And who knew what revolutionary and abolitionist turns a Republican government might take as the conflagration progressed? So, no, he told Blair in his courteous Virginia way, he could not fight against Virginia or the South, could not "raise my hand against my relatives, my children, my home." After that Lee had a talk with old Scott, also a Virginian, who lectured the colonel about his duty and patriotism. Then Lee rode back to Arlington.

The next Lincoln heard of him, Lee had taken command of the Virginia state troops and then enlisted in the Confederate Army, to fight for the preservation of slavery — the very thing he professed to oppose. In Lincoln's view, Lee was a strange and inexplicable man. Yet he was only one of many supposedly loyal Southern officers who violated their oaths of allegiance and went over to the rebels. Another Virginian, Captain John Bankhead Magruder of the artillery, came to see Lincoln, stood right here in his office and "repeated over and over again" his "protestations of loyalty," only to resign his commission and head for the South. It gave Lincoln the hypo. He referred to Lee, Magruder, and all like them as traitors.

So Lincoln must rely on Scott and his inexperienced junior officers. And for fighting men he must depend on the three-months militia he'd ordered up from the states. But where were they? Reports had come that some Pennsylvania units and the Sixth Massachusetts were on the march, but nobody knew when they would arrive. Only a skeleton force and a few ragtag volunteers now defended Washington. And rumors multiplied of impending rebel attack, of midnight assassinations and abduction plots which left Washington a vortex of fear. . . .

On Sunday, April 21 [1861], in an atmosphere of intense foreboding, Lincoln called his Cabinet Secretaries to an emergency meeting. With

Washington trapped between a secessionist Virginia and a hostile Maryland, they unanimously agreed that Lincoln must assume broad emergency powers or let the government fall. Accordingly he directed that Welles empower several private individuals — including Welles's own brother-in-law — to forward troops and supplies to embattled Washington. He allowed Cameron to authorize one Alexander Cummings and the governor of New York to transport troops and acquire supplies for the public defense. Because he thought the government was alive with traitors, Lincoln himself selected private citizens known for "their ability, loyalty, and patriotism" to spend public money without security, but without compensation either. He told Chase to advance two million dollars to three New Yorkers for the purpose of buying arms and making military preparations. Lincoln conceded that these emergency actions were "without authority of law," but argued that they were absolutely indispensable to save the government. And his Cabinet emphatically agreed.

Yet maybe even these measures were too late now. Two days passed and still no troops arrived. A White House staffer saw Lincoln pacing in his office, pausing from time to time to glance out the window. Why didn't the troops come? The governors of Indiana, Pennsylvania, Ohio, Illinois, New York, and Rhode Island had all promised to send thousands of men. Where were they? On April 24, a day "of gloom and doubt," Lincoln spoke with men of the Sixth Massachusetts in the White House. "I don't believe there is any North," Lincoln said. "*You* are the only Northern realities."

At last they came. At noon, April 25, the Seventh New York filed off a train in Washington and marched up Pennsylvania Avenue with snapping flags and a blaring band. The arrival of those troops gladdened Lincoln's heart, Hay said. In the next few days soldiers reached Washington by the hundreds, scrambling off steamers and trains from all over the North, until by April 27 some ten thousand were dug in along the Potomac and thousands more were on the way.

As though by a miracle, Washington was now transformed into an armed camp, with cavalry and caissons rumbling through the streets, barracks and hospitals springing up around the city, and tents dotting the landscape south of the capital, where men were renovating forts and throwing up earthworks. From the White House Lincoln could see soldiers everywhere on the sidewalks, could hear the staccato cry of bugles and the crack of musketry from army firing ranges.

As volunteers continued to stream in, here came none other than Elmer Ellsworth, leading a smart-looking Zouave outfit he'd raised in

New York. Young Ellsworth was dressed in a red cap and red shirt and was armed with a sword, a huge revolver, and an awesome bowie knife that could halve a man's head like an apple. The Lincolns gave him a warm reception in the White House, where he'd lived before going off to New York. In truth, he was so much a part of the family that he'd once caught the measles from Willie and Tad. For Lincoln, his boundless enthusiasm was a welcome relief from the dark days that had just passed.

As May came, a kind of heady optimism settled over Washington. Men talked about how the war would be over in ninety days. Military bands entertained Lincoln on sunny White House lawns; and couples rode out to picnic at the Great Falls. "You couldn't discover from anything but the everywhereness of uniforms and muskets," Nicolay said, "that we are in the midst of revolution and civil war."

In the springtime lull, with a fragrance of lilacs filling the White House, Lincoln and his Cabinet adopted a series of additional emergency measures designed to bring the rebellion to a speedy end. In a procession of orders and proclamations, the President declared a blockade of the Southern coast, added 22,000 men to the regular army and 18,000 to the navy, called for 42,000 three-year volunteers, and put national armories into full production. At the same time, he made certain that the Union war effort remained thoroughly bipartisan, handing out military commands to loyal Democrats as well as Republicans and summoning Union men of all political persuasions to help him save the government in this "great trouble."

Meanwhile, Lincoln dealt harshly with "the enemy in the rear" — with what he called "a most efficient corps of spies, informers, suppliers, and aiders and abettors" of the rebellion who took advantage of "Liberty of speech, Liberty of the press and *Habeas corpus*" to disrupt the Union war effort. Consequently he suspended the writ of habeas corpus and authorized army commanders to declare martial law in various areas behind the lines and to try civilians in military courts. Lincoln steadfastly defended such an invasion of civil liberties, contending that strict measures were imperative if the laws of the Union — and liberty itself — were to survive this "clear, flagrant, and gigantic case of Rebellion."

At the outset, responsibility for suppressing disloyal activities was divided among the State, War, and Navy departments, with Seward's State Department playing the largest role. Convinced that treason lurked everywhere, in every bureau, post office, customs house, regiment, and ship of war, Seward took extraordinary steps to root out subversives. He not only censored the telegraphs and the mails, but utilized government agents, United States marshals, Pinkerton's detectives, city police, and private informers to maintain surveillance of "suspicious" persons and to help arrest them. In May, Lincoln became apprehensive about such activities. "Unless the *necessity* for these arbitrary arrests is *manifest*, and *urgent*," he wrote in an executive memorandum, "I prefer they should cease."

So did Chief Justice Taney. While on circuit duty, he rebuked Lincoln for usurping power in suspending the writ of habeas corpus. Only Congress could legally do that, Taney argued, and he admonished the President not to violate the very laws he had sworn to uphold. "Are all the laws, *but one?* to go unexecuted," Lincoln replied later, in reference to habeas corpus, "and the government itself go to pieces, lest that one be violated?" Besides, the Constitution did not specify which branch of the government could suspend the writ, so that Lincoln didn't think he had broken any laws or violated his oath of office. Therefore the government would continue to imprison people who were known disloyalists. . . .

As summer approached, Lincoln found himself in the middle of a huge administrative mess, with every agency from the White House to the army in utter disarray. Never before had an administration had to cope with a massive insurrection or raise, equip, and supply such large field armies. Here was Lincoln, both inexperienced and unsystematic, having to solve complex problems for which precedents and guidelines were virtually nonexistent. His Cabinet members, moreover, lacked clear lines of authority in managing a civil war and often worked at cross-purposes and even interfered in one another's tasks. Welles, for his part, complained that Seward and Cameron meddled in navy matters as though Welles's office did not exist. And Chase, in addition to his Treasury chores, was as busy raising and inducting regiments into the army as was Cameron himself. Administratively, Washington was a whirlwind of confusion and chaos.

The worst troubles were in Cameron's War Department, where a minuscule staff tried in vain to direct the military colossus now being assembled. In truth, there was such a swell of patriotism and surge of volunteering across the Union, with Republicans and Democrats alike swamping military centers, that the understaffed War Department could not possibly accommodate or even keep track of all the regiments arriving in Washington each day. And Simon Cameron, as confused as he was injudicious, sometimes refused to accept state regiments, which sent both governors and officers squalling at Lincoln. As if he didn't have enough minutiae to worry about already, in addition to fashioning national and international policies, now he had to tend to individual regiments as well. He hated to interfere with his Cabinet Secretaries in their duties, but in the case of rejected regiments he did. Time and again he sent over memoranda advising Cameron to take the latest outfits offered from Massachusetts, from Indiana and Michigan. When rival recruiters quarreled over whose units should be enlisted, Lincoln told Cameron to induct them all.

What a headache it was to build an army. Not only did Lincoln have to contend with unhappy recruiters; he also had to sign hundreds of officers' commissions in both the regular and the volunteer armies. And he had to allot so many generalships to each state and fill each position himself. The result was a plethora of "political generals," as Lincoln handed out commissions to both Republicans and Democrats — to men like James Shields of Illinois (Lincoln's old dueling opponent) and Nathaniel Banks and Benjamin Butler of Massachusetts. Why let politicians become officers? "To keep them from fighting against the war with their mouths," a Lincoln friend explained. Still, the dual army system, which piled layers of volunteers on top of the regular army nucleus, only added to the growing military jumble. To make matters worse, there were shortages of everything from shoes to guns. "The plain matter-of-fact is," a harried Lincoln wrote one officer, "our good people have rushed to the rescue of the Government, faster than the government can find arms to put into their hands." And finding military supplies led to still more bureaucratic tangles. Because his department was understaffed, Cameron turned to state governors and private citizens for help. The result was widespread disorder, as agents representing governors as well as the Ordnance, Quartermaster, and Commissary bureaus of the War Department vied with one another in spending federal funds for war matériel.

Then there was the Negro problem, haunting Lincoln as always. Caught up like whites in the rush of patriotism, black men across the North wanted to fight for the country as their forebears had done in the Revolution and the War of 1812. The trouble was that a federal law now barred Negroes from enrolling in state militias, and the all-white regular army was not about to accept any blacks. Even so, Negroes in various cities organized their own outfits and set about drilling until white authorities made them stop. When blacks urged the administration to let them serve, Lincoln told them no. As both the *Illinois State Journal* and the *New York Tribune* said, this was strictly a white man's war.

It was also strictly a war to save the Union and not to free the slaves, as Lincoln repeatedly asserted. Yet slavery was inextricably involved in the conflict — was the reason the South had seceded in the first place — and was bound to create a problem wherever Union troops touched rebel territory. For example: at the tip of Virginia's Yorktown peninsula, where General Butler now commanded Fort Monroe, fugitive slaves were flocking to his lines. And rebel whites were demanding their return, as though they were still protected by the laws of the very government from which they had seceded and which they were now resisting by force of arms. Butler refused to hand the blacks over and pronounced them "contraband of war," which seemed only a few steps shy of emancipating them.

Lincoln was concerned about Butler's action, for he did not want this misconstrued as emancipation. He feared that the slightest move in that direction would alienate Northern Democrats and send the critical border spiraling into the Confederacy. No, his policy was to remain consistent with Republican promises and to bring the South back with the peculiar institution still intact. Nevertheless, after talking the matter over with the Cabinet, he approved of Butler's move. The fugitive slave law no longer applied to those in rebellion against the government and their slaves need not be returned. After that, word spread across the slave grapevine from Virginia to Tennessee; and many a slave, after running through the woods all night, reached Union lines and said, "I'se contraband." . . .

By the summer of 1861, Lincoln's day had become a set routine. After a "sleep light and capricious," he rose at first light and was at work in his office by seven. His "shop," as he called it, was a large room on the second floor of the White House. It contained a marble fireplace, two hair-covered sofas, a big oak table for Cabinet meetings, and a desk with documents and correspondence stuffed in pigeonholes. On the wall were framed military maps and a faded oil painting of Andrew Jackson. Lincoln usually wrote at a table between two high windows, sitting in a large armchair with his legs crossed. This June he worked on his message to Congress, writing in his usual slow and laborious manner, often whispering phrases to get them right before he wrote them down. From time to time he would pause to stare out the windows, which afforded a sweeping view of the south lawn, the Smithsonian Institution, the unfinished Washington monument, and the distant Virginia hills, covered now with Union tents, wagon trains, and bawling cattle.

At nine he breakfasted with his family, downing an egg and a cup of coffee, and then returned to the shop with callers already assembling downstairs. For an hour or so he studied a digest of the day's news prepared by his personal secretaries, Nicolay and Hay, and discussed important correspondence. Nicolay (or "Nico") was twenty-nine now, an emaciated fellow with blue eyes and a slow smile, who wrote love letters to a girl back in Illinois. Hay, at twenty-three, was a boyish gadfly who loved wine and cheese and laughed compulsively at anything. Both young men idolized Lincoln, would do anything for him, and would one day write an encyclopedic history of his administration. For Mary Lincoln, though, they had nothing but adamant hostility. They did not understand what pressures and hurts lay behind her temper flares, and with youthful intolerance they disparaged her as a raging "Hellcat" whose shrieks made the White House tremble.

Nicolay and Hay did their best to guard Lincoln from intruders, cranks, and politicians who tried to push past them to see "the new man," but Lincoln was hard to protect. At first he placed no limits on visitors, and they accosted him incessantly from dawn to dusk, making it impossible for him to tend his other chores. So with Nicolay and Hay the President worked out a system: he would see people on Monday, Wednesday, and Friday from ten till two, on Tuesday and Thursday from ten till noon, when he was supposed to meet with the Cabinet. His personal secretaries, situated in an adjacent office, were to head off anybody who tried to interrupt him other than during office hours. With a system thus established, Lincoln proceeded to "break through every regulation as fast as it was made," his secretaries complained. If they told some caller to come back during regular hours, Lincoln would open his door and invite the person in anyway. It infuriated Nicolay and Hay. How could there be an office system if Lincoln ignored the system? The trouble was that Lincoln loathed rules and red tape and generally did as he wanted, as though the White House were his Springfield law office.

Officially, Lincoln would throw his door open at ten and let in a river of raucous humanity — interviewers, politicians, office seekers, businessmen, sobbing mothers who wanted their sons released from the army, and pretty young wives who flirted with him to promote their military husbands. At times Lincoln enjoyed all the attention he received — particularly from the young women. And he was courteous and attentive to most everyone — the jobless, the infirm, the promoters, the parvenus — who passed through his doors. He avoided false enthusiasms, never lied and exclaimed "I am delighted to see you" when he wasn't delighted. Usually he would greet people with "What can I do for you?" Then he would listen, stroking his beard, and would promise to do what he could if the request were reasonable. If he was in a hurry to get rid of someone, he would crack a joke and with both of them laughing would ease the caller out the door. Sensitive himself, he tried to give everybody something, if only "a quaint phrase" or a memorable poem. Once he recited an entire poem of Oliver Wendell Holmes to a group of enchanted ladies.

Still, some visitors thought him less a man of culture and polished wit than a shrewd "old codger" like Andrew Jackson. A New York lawyer was astonished at Lincoln's language, reporting that he said "thar" for *there*, "git" for *get*, "kin" for *can*, "one of 'em" for *one of them*, and "I hain't been caught lyin' yet, and I don't mean to be."

Lincoln claimed to like his "public opinion baths," deemed them an indispensable way of finding out what people were thinking. But sometimes the crowds and the endless demands were too much, his temper would blaze, and he would call somebody "a damned rascal" or explode at a persistent visitor: "Now go away! I can't attend to all these details. I could as easily bail out the Potomac with a teaspoon." In truth, the long visitations wore him out. He complained about "the numerous grist ground through here daily," from some senator desiring a war with France to some poor woman after a Treasury job, and remarked that each caller took away a special piece of his vitality. "When I get through with such a day's work," he sighed, "there is only one word which can express my condition, and that is — *flabbiness*." Nicolay and Hay estimated that he spent three-fourths of his time meeting with people. The crowds were so great that sometimes even U.S. senators had to wait ten days to see him.

One class of visitors Lincoln always welcomed. These were inventors and gunsmiths who came to promote some newfangled weapon. Fascinated with the tools of war, Lincoln loved to examine and talk about them. Whenever he could, he would slip away from the morning crowds and witness the testing of some new gun out at the firing ranges. One day he took Hay down to the Navy Yard to watch ordnance experts test fire the great Dahlgren gun into the Potomac. The cannon exploded with a tremendous concussion and the eleven-inch shell ricocheted across the water like a thrown boulder, churning up a thirty-foot column of spray with every jump, until at last it rolled over in the waves. "The President," Hay said, "was delighted." On other mornings, Lincoln might go over to his private rifle range, in the Treasury Park beyond the south lawn, and fire some new rifle himself, blazing away at a target pinned to a woodpile there. The President not only tried out the new breach-loading rifle, which he thought superior to the muzzle-loaders used by the army, but helped in its eventual introduction into his armed forces. He was also instrumental in the development and introduction of a rudimentary machine gun. . . .

Sometime in the afternoon Lincoln would run "the gauntlet" down to the family rooms in the West Wing and have a biscuit and a glass of milk for lunch. Midafternoon found him back in his shop doing paper work — signing commissions, composing important letters, sending out memos to various department heads about requests received that morning, asking Chase to look into this, Cameron into that. "The lady — bearer of this — says she has two sons who want to work," Lincoln wrote on one memo. "Set them at it, if possible. Wanting to work is so rare a merit, that it should be encouraged."

At four he would get away from the White House and go for a carriage ride — his only regular source of relaxation. Sometimes Mary would accompany him. If she were out of town, then Seward or an old Illinois crony would go along. Often they would rattle across the Washington bridge to review troops in Virginia, visit officers in their quarters, chat with the men at army messes, with the odor of biscuits and pork in the wind. Then they would head through the woods, enjoying the fresh air, the cawing birds, the tangle of limbs against the June sky. To guard against assassination, a cavalry escort accompanied Lincoln on his country rides, although he protested all security measures as a nuisance. Why would anybody want to kill him? What could that possibly gain? And in any event, anybody who really wanted to shoot him could do it with or without a military patrol. When mounted guards and infantry were detailed to protect the White House, Lincoln dismissed them because they made him feel like an emperor. But he grudgingly consented to the cavalry escort for his carriage rides, even though they made such a racket with their jingling spurs and clanging sabers that he and his companion could scarcely hear one another. The story goes that Lincoln liked to prod his coachman and try to outrun the cavalry — the President's carriage careening down dusty roads, the flustered soldiers trying in vain to catch him.

Then it was back to the White House for dinner at six. Usually Lincoln dined with his family and a few friends or special guests. State dinners, wretchedly formal affairs, began at seven-thirty, and Lincoln ate lightly from one or two courses, took a sip of wine, and then joined the men in the sitting rooms, though he abstained from the cigars and brandy. Once or twice a week there were evening dress receptions, or levees, when he had to greet a flood of people in a capacious White House room. Herman Melville met him on one such occasion and said he shook hands "like a man sawing wood at so much per cord." The levees, too, were painful ordeals which left his right hand so swollen and sore that he could not use it for hours.

On rare evenings when there were no receptions and no pressing work to do, Lincoln would relax with Seward and a small circle of Illinois associates — men like Browning or Ward Hill Lamon, now United States marshal of Washington, D.C. To ease the exhaustion of the day, Lincoln would let his humor flow, until "he was once more the Lincoln of the Eighth Circuit," Hay said, "the cheeriest of talkers, the riskiest of story tellers." When he reached his punch line, observed one visitor, Lincoln "wrinkled up his nose" and "showing all his front teeth gave a very wheezy catching laugh and in his glee fell to scratching himself on the elbows."

His White House tales gave rise to a new item called "Lincoln stories," but Lincoln always denied their originality. "You speak of Lincoln's stories," he once told a correspondent. "I don't think that is a correct phrase. I don't make the stories mine by telling them. I am only a retail dealer." Yet he conceded that humor was his therapy. "Some of the stories are not so nice as they might be, but I tell you the truth when I say that a funny story, if it has the element of genuine wit, has the same effect on me that I suppose a good square drink of whiskey has on an old toper; it puts new life into me."

The opera and theater restored him, too. Whenever he could spare the time, he and Mary would dress up, climb into the Presidential carriage, and sally forth into the Washington night to attend one of several theaters. Mary loved the theater more than any other form of entertainment. And Lincoln considered it a "wonderful" way to escape the troubles of his office. He preferred Shakespearean productions — not the tragedies, which he liked to read, but the comedies with their risqué scenes and pungent dialogue. Lincoln enjoyed almost any humorous play, "no matter how absurd or grotesque." He was even delighted with John Brougham's "travesty" of *Pocahontas*, and cracked puns and chortled at its "delicious absurdity." If Mary were out of town, Lincoln would often slip out alone to see a play or go to the opera. Or he might take Hay to a concert, for he liked music of all kinds, from military bands to dancing choruses. At one concert in Ford's Theater, he and young Hay amused themselves in a private box, applauding the singers and carrying on "a hefty flirtation with the M — Girls in the flies."

For Lincoln, though, a night out was rare. He spent most evenings in his White House office, working late into the night, toiling on his Congressional speech or some other composition. In the summer he had to raise the windows, which let in waves of insects to buzz around the lamps and flutter against the walls. And then there were the awful smells, wafting in from drainage ditches and the unreclaimed Potomac flats, a stench Hay likened to that of "twenty thousand drowned cats." After a June shower came squadrons of mosquitoes, which spread malarial fevers through the White House until most everyone there shook and cried from the ague.

To escape the mosquitoes and sweltering Washington heat, the Lincolns retreated up to the Retired Soldiers' Home, situated in the woods a couple of miles to the northwest. Here the elevation was higher and the nights cooler than down in the capital. Mary thought the Soldiers' Home "a very beautiful place" where "we can be as secluded, as we please," so the Lincolns moved into a cottage on the grounds and it became a summer White House. In the mornings Lincoln would ride alone into Washington to spend his whirlwind days, then would return at night to relax in cool seclusion with his family. Here, when Mary and the boys were asleep, he would do his late-night work by lamplight. Later, while waiting for sleep to come, he would read his worn copy of Shakespeare's tragedies, turning again and again to *Hamlet* and *Macbeth*. Or he might peruse a volume of poetry — of Burns, Whittier, or Holmes — and recite half aloud those sad and pathetic stanzas he knew by heart and loved so well. "Green be the graves where her martyrs are lying! Shroudless and tombless they sunk to their rest . . . " It was the beginning of a stanza from Holmes which moved Lincoln almost as much as "Mortality." Then at last, when all was quiet except for the groan of trees in the wind, Lincoln would sink into a restless sleep, often filled with dream sequences about war and distant voices and a phantom ship moving in the fog.

Questions for Discussion

1.   Abraham Lincoln assumed greater emergency powers than any other American president. A keen student of the Framers and of the philosophers on whose ideas the Constitution was based, he was convinced that the Constitution permitted him to take extraordinary actions to prevent its very destruction. What are the dangers of such an interpretation of the Constitution, and do you think Lincoln overstepped his limits in prosecuting the Civil War?

2.   Lincoln often argued that the Civil War was in fact a great domestic rebellion, not a war between two sovereign nations, and that it was primarily about saving the Union — not about extinguishing slavery. Why do you think he favored this interpretation of the conflict? What were the political costs and benefits of such a rationale?

3.   Stephen Oates illustrates that, although Lincoln governed during the most perilous period in the Republic's history, he took strength and succor from the brief interludes of levity and relaxation. What does his approach to the daily rigors of his job tell you about his character, and perhaps about how people are capable of balancing supremely difficult tasks with the more routine facets of life?

8 When the Laws Were Silent

WILLIAM H. REHNQUIST

We saw earlier (selection #7) that at the start of the Civil War, President Lincoln curtailed some civil liberties — very unpopular decisions at the time. To Lincoln, morality of action was found in "preserving the nation." "Defending the nation" was President Franklin D. Roosevelt's imperative. The movement to put thousands of Americans of Japanese ancestry into internment camps originated with the State of California, was supported by popular opinion, traveled through various executive departments in Washington, and ultimately landed on the desk of a president busy with the details of winning a war. Chief Justice William Rehnquist considers this curtailment of civil liberties through three related decisions of the Supreme Court.

THE ENTIRE NATION was stunned by the Japanese attack on Pearl Harbor on December 7, 1941, but it seemed much closer to home on the West Coast than elsewhere on the mainland. Residents became fearful of ethnic Japanese among them. Japanese immigrants had begun to settle on the West Coast shortly before the turn of the century and had not been assimilated into the rest of the population. Under the Naturalization Act of 1790, those who had emigrated from Japan were not able to become citizens; they were prohibited by law from owning land and were socially segregated in many ways. The first generation of Japanese immigrants, the issei, therefore remained aliens. But their children, the nisei, having been born in the United States, were citizens from birth. Californians particularly, including public officials — Gov. Culbert Olson, State Attorney General Earl Warren, and the mayor of Los Angeles, Fletcher Bowron — began to call for "relocation" to the interior of the country of persons of Japanese ancestry. At the outbreak of the war the military established the Western Defense Command, which included the coastal portions of California, Oregon, and Washington. Gen. John

DeWitt, its senior officer, at first resisted the clamor to remove the Japanese. But state and local public officials were adamant, and they were supported by their states' congressional delegations. The chorus became more insistent when the Roberts Commission released its report in late January 1942.

On December 18, 1941, President Roosevelt had appointed a body chaired by Owen J. Roberts, an Associate Justice of the Supreme Court, "to ascertain and report the facts relating to the attack made by Japanese armed forces upon the territory of Hawaii on December 7, 1941." The commission met first in Washington and then went to Hawaii, where the members heard numerous witnesses. The commission found that there had been highly organized espionage in Hawaii: "it has been discovered that the Japanese consul sent to and received from Tokyo in his own and other names many messages on commercial radio circuits. This activity greatly increased towards December 7, 1941. . . . [The Japanese] knew from maps which they had obtained, the exact location of vital air fields, hangars, and other structures. They also knew accurately where certain important naval vessels would be berthed. Their fliers had the most detailed maps, courses, and bearings, so that each could attack a given vessel or field. Each seems to have been given a specified mission."

In February 1942 a Japanese submarine shelled oil installations near Santa Barbara. The pressure built for forced evacuation. Attorney General Francis Biddle, Secretary of War Henry L. Stimson, and Assistant Secretary of War John J. McCloy were the decision-makers for the two concerned departments. None of them favored relocation at first, but eventually Stimson and McCloy changed their minds in the course of often heated discussions among themselves and their subordinates. Final approval of course rested with the President. On February 11, 1942, McCloy asked Stimson to find out if Roosevelt was willing to authorize the removal of the nisei as well as the issei. Stimson asked to see the President but was told FDR was too busy; a phone call would have to do. "I took up with him the West Coast matter first," Stimson wrote in his diary, "and told him the situation and fortunately found he was very vigorous about it and told me to go ahead on the line that I had myself thought the best."

Then, Stimson wrote in his 1947 memoirs, "mindful of its duty to be prepared for any emergency, the War Department ordered the evacuation of more than a hundred thousand persons of Japanese origin from strategic areas on the west coast. This decision was widely criticized as an unconstitutional invasion of the rights of individuals many of whom were American citizens, but it was eventually approved by the Supreme Court as a legitimate exercise of the war powers of the President. What critics ignored was the situation that led to the evacuation. Japanese raids on the west coast seemed not only possible but probable in the first months of the war, and it was quite impossible to be sure that the raiders would not receive important help from individuals of Japanese origin."

Biddle, who alone among the high administration officials involved opposed the evacuation, described the situation in these words: "Apparently, the War Department's course of action had been tentatively charted by Mr. McCloy and Colonel Karl Robin Bendetsen of the General Staff in the first ten days of February. General DeWitt's final recommendation to evacuate was completed on February 13, and forwarded to Washington with a covering letter the next day. Mr. Stimson and Mr. McCloy did not, however, wait for this report, which contained the 'finding' on which their 'military necessity' argument to the President was based, but obtained their authority before the recommendation was received. On February 11 the President told the War Department to prepare a plan for wholesale evacuation, specifically including citizens. It was dictated, he concluded, by military necessity, and added, 'Be as reasonable as you can.' After the conference the Assistant Secretary reported to Bendetsen: 'We have carte blanche to do what we want as far as the President is concerned.' " Biddle speculated on Roosevelt's feelings about the matter: "I do not think he was much concerned with the gravity or implications of this step. He was never theoretical about things. What must be done to defend the country must be done." Biddle concluded with a remarkably perceptive observation: "Nor do I think that the constitutional difficulty plagued him — the Constitution has never greatly bothered any wartime President. That was a question of law, which ultimately the Supreme Court must decide. And meanwhile — probably a long meanwhile — we must get on with the war."

Executive Order 9066, authorizing the removal of the ethnic Japanese from the West Coast, was signed by Roosevelt on February 19. Several weeks later Congress passed a law imposing criminal penalties for violations of the order or regulations that might be issued to implement it. First a curfew was imposed on the ethnic Japanese, then they were required to report to relocation centers, and finally they were taken to camps in the interior of California and in the mountain states. There was no physical brutality, but there were certainly severe hardships: removal from the place where one lived, often the forced sale of houses and businesses, and harsh living conditions in the Spartan quarters of the internment centers. As the war progressed, some restrictions were relaxed. Nisei volunteers made up the 442d Combat Team, which fought bravely in Italy against the Germans. Other internees were issued work permits that allowed them to leave the camp. Finally, most of those who were still interned were released by the beginning of 1945, as a result of the third Supreme Court decision in which the relocation policy was challenged.

Gordon Hirabayashi was born near Seattle to issei parents in 1918, and by 1942 he was a senior at the University of Washington. In May 1942 he disobeyed the curfew requirement imposed by military authorities pursuant to the President's Executive Order, and seven days later he failed to report to register for evacuation. He was indicted and convicted in a federal court in Seattle on two misdemeanor counts and sentenced to imprisonment for three months on each. He contended that the orders he was charged with violating were unconstitutional, but the federal judge in Seattle ruled against him. Fred Korematsu, born in the United States to issei parents, was convicted of remaining in San Leandro, California, in violation of a military exclusion order applicable to him. The federal court in San Francisco overruled his claim that the order in question was unconstitutional, suspended his sentence, and placed him on probation for five years.

The cases were argued together before the U.S. Court of Appeals for the Ninth Circuit in San Francisco, which has jurisdiction over the Far Western part of the United States. Because of procedural variations, they reached the Supreme Court at different times. The case of Hirabayashi was sent directly there by the court of appeals and was argued in May 1943. . . .

The Japanese-Americans were represented in the Supreme Court by able counsel, including Edwin Borchard, William Draper Lewis, Brien McMahon, and Osmond K. Fraenkel. Their basic contention was that the President's Executive Order was unconstitutional because it proceeded on the basis that an entire racial group was disloyal, rather than being based on any individual determinations of disloyalty. Briefs supporting these petitioners were filed by the American Civil Liberties Union, the Northern California branch of the American Civil Liberties Union, and the Japanese American Citizens League.

The government in its brief recited in great detail the calamitous military events of the early days of the war—these ranged from the Pearl Harbor raid to the fall of the British stronghold of Singapore, which it thought justified the orders now being challenged, and went on to catalogue the "concentration of war facilities and installations on the West Coast [that] made it an area of special military concern at any time and especially after the sensational Japanese successes."

The attorneys general of Washington, Oregon, and California filed a brief in support of the government that pointed out that "for the first seven months little occurred to reduce the fear of attack. . . . On June 3, 1942, Dutch Harbor, Alaska, was attacked by carrier-based planes. On June 7, 1942, the Japanese invaded continental North America by occupying the Islands of Attu and Kiska in the Aleutian group. There was an increasing indication that the enemy had knowledge of our patrols and naval dispositions, for ships leaving west coast ports were being intercepted and attacked regularly by enemy submarines." Following the oral argument and conference in the Hirabayashi case, Chief Justice Stone assigned the task of writing the Court's opinion to himself. He first greatly narrowed the scope of the opinion by deciding that the Court need pass only on the validity of the curfew requirement and not on the requirement that Hirabayashi report to a relocation center. Hirabayashi had been convicted of both offenses, but his sentences were to run "concurrently" — that is, he would serve only three months in prison even though he had been sentenced to serve three months on each of two different charges. Under established law at that time, if the conviction on one count was upheld, the Court would disregard the conviction on the second count, since it essentially made no difference in the amount of time the defendant would spend in prison. In this case it meant that the Court had to tackle only the easier question of whether a curfew might be imposed, rather than the more difficult one of whether Hirabayashi could be sent to an internment camp. . . .

Stone's opinion for the Court borrowed a definition of the government's war power from a statement made by Charles Evans Hughes — not while he was a member of the Court but in an article in the American Bar Association Journal: The war power of the national government is "the power to wage war successfully," and it was "not for any court to sit in review of the wisdom of their [the Executive's or Congress's] actions, or to substitute its judgment for theirs." If the Court could say there was a rational basis for the military decision, it would be sustained.

Stone's opinion then adduced the facts — most of which had been set forth in the government's brief — that showed the threat by the Japanese Navy to the Pacific Coast immediately after the Pearl Harbor bombing. It went on to say: "Whatever views we may entertain regarding the loyalty to this country of the citizens of Japanese ancestry, we cannot reject as unfounded the judgment of the military authorities and of Congress that there were disloyal members of that population, whose number and strength could not be precisely and quickly ascertained. We cannot say that the war-making branches of the Government did not have ground for believing that in a critical hour such persons could not readily be isolated and separately dealt with, and constituted a menace to the national defense and safety, which demanded that prompt and adequate measures be taken to guard against it."

The Court, of course, had to respond to the charge that distinctions based on race alone were not permitted under the Constitution: "Distinctions between citizens solely because of their ancestry are by their very nature odious to a free people whose institutions are founded upon the doctrine of equality. . . . We may assume that these considerations would be controlling here were it not for the fact that the danger of espionage and sabotage, in time of war and of threatened invasion, calls upon the military authorities to scrutinize every relevant fact bearing on the loyalty of populations in the danger areas. . . . The fact alone that the attack on our shores was threatened by Japan rather than another enemy power set these citizens apart from others who have no particular associations with Japan." Stone's opinion upholding the curfew was joined by five of his colleagues. Douglas, Murphy, and Rutledge, while voting to uphold the curfew, wrote separately.

Korematsu's case did not come on for argument until October 1944. Here the Court was required to confront not merely the curfew but the far more draconian relocation requirement. The Court upheld relocation, in an opinion by Justice Black, basing its reasoning largely on the earlier decision. This time, however, there were separate dissents by Justices Roberts, Murphy, and Jackson. The flavor of Black's opinion is caught in its concluding passage: "To cast this case into outlines of racial prejudice, without reference to the real military dangers which were presented, merely confuses the issue. Korematsu was not excluded from the Military Area because of hostility to him or his race. He was excluded because we are at war with the Japanese Empire, because the properly constituted military authorities feared an invasion of our West Coast and felt constrained to take proper security measures, because they decided that the military urgency of the situation demanded that all citizens of Japanese ancestry be segregated from the West Coast temporarily. . . . There was evidence of disloyalty on the part of some, the military authorities considered that the need for action was great, and time was short. We cannot — by availing ourselves of the calm perspective of hindsight — now say that at that time these actions were unjustified."

Murphy criticized the military for lumping together with a disloyal few of Japanese ancestry all the others against whom there had been no such showing. Jackson said that the Court was simply in no position to evaluate the government's claim of military necessity: "In the very nature of things, military decisions are not susceptible of intelligent judicial appraisal. They do not pretend to rest on evidence, but are made on information that often would not be admissible and on assumptions that could not be proved. . . . Hence courts can never have any real alternative to accepting the mere declaration of the authority that issued the order that it was reasonably necessary from a military viewpoint."

But in the case of Endo, argued and decided at the same time as Korematsu, the Court reached quite a different result. Mitsuye Endo had submitted to an evacuation order and been removed first to the Tule Lake Relocation Center in the Cascade Mountains just south of the California-Oregon border and then to another relocation center in Utah. She sued out a writ of habeas corpus, claiming that she was a loyal citizen against whom no charge had been made and that she was therefore entitled to her relief. The government agreed that she was a loyal citizen and not charged with any offense. The Court decided that under these circumstances Endo was entitled to be released from confinement. The presidential order and the act of Congress confirming it spoke of evacuation from a military zone but said nothing of detention after the evacuation. While the initial evacuation had been justified in terms of the defense facilities on the West Coast, the detention of a loyal person of Japanese ancestry after the evacuation had taken place was not reasonably necessary to prevent sabotage or espionage. Two members of the Court wrote separately, but all agreed with the result. . . .

There is a certain disingenuousness in this sequence of three opinions — Hirabayashi, Korematsu, and Endo. There was no reason to think that Gordon Hirabayashi and Fred Korematsu were any less loyal to the United States than was Mitsuye Endo. Presumably they would have been entitled to relief from detention upon the same showing as that made by Endo. But even had Hirabayashi tried to raise that question in his case, he would have failed, for the Court chose to confine itself to the curfew issue. It was not until we were clearly winning the war that the Court came around to this view in Endo. The process illustrates in a rough way the Latin maxim *Inter arma silent leges* [in time of war the laws are silent].

Postwar public opinion very quickly came to see the forced relocation and detention of people of Japanese ancestry as a grave injustice. Writing in 1945, Eugene Rostow, then a professor at Yale Law School and later its dean, declared the program "a disaster" that both represented an abandonment of our traditional subordination of military to civil authority and sanctioned racially based discrimination. Edward Ennis, who as a lawyer in the Justice Department had opposed the program, reappeared nearly forty years later on behalf of the ACLU to testify before the

congressionally created Commission on Wartime Relocation and Internment of Civilians. He characterized the program as "the worst blow to
civil liberty in our history." In the view of this author, some of this
criticism is well justified, and some not; its principal fault is that it lumps
together the cases of the issei and the nisei.

The cases before the Supreme Court — Hirabayashi, Korematsu, and
Endo — all involved nisei, children of immigrants, who were born in the
United States and thus were American. The basis on which the Court
upheld the plan were military representations as to the necessity for
evacuation. These representations were undoubtedly exaggerated, and
they were based in part on the view that not only the issei but their
children were different from other West Coast residents.

In defense of the military it should be pointed out that these officials
were not entrusted with the protection of anyone's civil liberty; their job
was making sure that vital areas were as secure as possible from espionage
or sabotage. The role of General DeWitt was not one to encourage a
nice calculation of the costs in civil liberty as opposed to the benefits to
national security. Gen. Walter Short, the Army commander in Hawaii,
and Adm. Husband E. Kimmel, the Navy commander there, both were
summarily removed from their commands ten days after Pearl Harbor
because of their failure to anticipate the Japanese surprise attack. The
head of the Western Defense command was surely going to err on the
side of preparedness.

Moreover, it was not DeWitt and his associates who had first recommended evacuation of the issei and nisei; as we have seen, the principal
early proponents of that idea were Governor Olson, Attorney General
Warren, Los Angeles Mayor Bowron, and the congressional delegations
of the three West Coast states. Public opinion should not be the determining factor in making a military appraisal, but it is bound to occur to
those engaged in that task how they will be regarded if they reject a
widely popular security measure that in retrospect turns out to have been
necessary.

The United States prides itself on having a system in which the
civilian heads of the service departments are supreme over the military
chiefs, so one might expect that Henry Stimson and John McCloy would
have made a more careful evaluation of the evacuation proposal than they
appear to have done. Far from the Pacific Coast, they would be expected
to have a more detached view than the commander on the scene. But
here too there seems to have been a tendency to feel that concern for
civil liberty was not their responsibility. There is even more of this feeling
in Roosevelt's perfunctory approval of the plan in response to a phone

call from Stimson. Biddle's protests proved futile even at the highest levels of government, in part because no significant element of public opinion opposed the relocation.

Once the relocation plan was in place, it could be challenged only in the courts. Was the Supreme Court at fault in upholding first the curfew, in Hirabayashi, and then the relocation, in Korematsu? In Hirabayashi the Court could have decided both the validity of the relocation requirement and the curfew requirement, for the "concurrent sentence" doctrine under which it declined to do so is discretionary. But counseling against any broader decision was the well-established rule that the Court should avoid deciding constitutional questions if at all possible, and so the Hirabayashi decision left the far more difficult question for another day.

When that day came, in Korematsu, a majority of the Court upheld the relocation program. Justice Black's opinion for the Court in Korematsu followed the same line of reasoning as had Chief Justice Stone's in Hira-bayashi. But this time there were three dissenters, who had voted to uphold the curfew but wanted to strike down the relocation program.

Over the years, several criticisms have been made of the Court's opinions in these cases. The most general is of its extremely deferential treatment given to the government's argument that the curfew and reloca-tion were necessitated by military considerations. Here one can only echo Justice Jackson's observation that "in the very nature of things, military decisions are not susceptible of intelligent judicial appraisal." But it surely does not follow from this that a court must therefore invalidate measures based on military judgments. Eugene Rostow suggested holding a judicial inquiry into the entire question of military necessity, but this seems an extraordinarily dubious proposition. Judicial inquiry, with its restrictive rules of evidence, orientation toward resolution of factual disputes in individual cases, and long delays, is ill suited to determine an urgent issue. The necessity for prompt action was cogently stated by the Court in its Hirabayashi opinion: "Although the results of the attack on Pearl Harbor were not fully disclosed until much later, it was known that the damage was extensive, and that the Japanese by their successes had gained a naval superiority over our forces in the Pacific which might enable them to seize Pearl Harbor, our largest naval base and the last stronghold of defense lying between Japan and the west coast. That reasonably prudent men charged with the responsibility of our national defense had ample ground for concluding that they must face the danger of invasion, take measures against it, and in making the choice of measures consider our internal situation, cannot be doubted."

The second criticism is that the decisions in these cases upheld a program that, at bottom, was based on racial distinctions. There are several levels at which this criticism can be made. The broadest is that the nisei were relocated simply because the Caucasian majority on the West Coast (and in the country as a whole) disliked them and wished to remove them as neighbors or as business competitors. The Court's answer to this attack seems satisfactory: Those of Japanese descent were displaced because of fear that disloyal elements among them would aid Japan in the war. Though there were undoubtedly nativists in California who welcomed a chance to see the issei and the nisei removed, it does not follow that this point of view was attributable to the military decisionmakers. They, after all, did not at first propose relocation. But a narrower criticism along the same line has more force to it: The nisei were evacuated notwithstanding the fact that they were American citizens. Even in wartime citizens may not be rounded up and required to prove their loyalty. They may be excluded from sensitive military areas in the absence of a security clearance and otherwise be denied access to any classified information, but it pushes these propositions to an extreme to say that a sizable geographic area, including the homes of many citizens, may be declared off-limits and the residents forced to move. It pushes it to an even greater extreme to say that such persons may be required not only to leave their homes but to report to and remain in a distant relocation center. . . .

An entirely separate and important philosophical question is whether occasional presidential excesses and judicial restraint in wartime are desirable or undesirable. In one sense this question is very largely academic. There is no reason to think that future wartime Presidents will act differently from Roosevelt or that future Justices of the Supreme Court will decide questions differently from their predecessors. It is neither desirable nor remotely likely that civil liberty will occupy as favored a position in wartime as it does in peacetime.

But it is both desirable and likely that the courts will pay more careful attention to the basis for the government's claims of necessity as a reason for curtailing civil liberty. The laws will thus not be silent in time of war, even though they will speak with a somewhat different voice.

Questions for Discussion

1. Did President Franklin Roosevelt and the government formulate the policy toward Japanese-Americans primarily on the basis of national security or nationalism and racism?

2.   Assess the dilemma the Supreme Court faces as it weighs the protection of society against the rights of the individual. How should the Court determine which set of values it should favor in a particular case?

3.   What do you think would happen today if an American president sought to place a particular ethnic group of American citizens into confinement? Can you imagine circumstances in which the American people would support such an action? Would and should the courts be more willing to question the government's logic for taking such steps?

9 No Ordinary Time: Franklin and Eleanor Roosevelt: The Home Front in World War II

DORIS KEARNS GOODWIN

World War II was "no ordinary time," notes historian Doris Kearns Goodwin as she relates how President Franklin Roosevelt and First Lady Eleanor Roosevelt dealt with the many problems of a nation at war. Here, Goodwin assesses Roosevelt and his administration's decisions concerning the plight of European Jews. Was enough done to try to save them from Hitler's concentration camps? Did Roosevelt's leadership of the war effort justify his lack of intervention?

WHILE AMERICANS FRETTED over the plight of British children who were not yet in danger, the people who most urgently needed help were the Jewish refugees from Germany who were trapped in Vichy France. One of the provisions in the French armistice agreement required the Vichy government to return on demand all German citizens named by the German government. As American ships crossed the Atlantic to save the British children, Gestapo agents were on their way to France to round up every German Jewish man, woman, and child they could find. But when Congressman William Schulte of Indiana tried to broaden the use of the visitor visas to any European child under sixteen, his bill was killed before it even reached the floor. The crucial difference, in terms of American public opinion, between the British and the German children was that the British boys and girls were mostly Christian, the German children mostly Jewish.

Throughout the 1930s, as tens of thousands of Jews fled Nazi Germany, Roosevelt worked behind the scenes to let more people in. Estimates show that, in the years between 1933 and 1940, nearly 105,000 refugees from Nazism reached safety in the United States, a record, though limited, that went beyond that of any other country. Only Palestine, which took in 55,000 during these same years, approached the American figure.

But those who were granted refuge were pitifully few compared with those who were trying to flee. "The long pathetic list of refugee ships, unable to find harbors open to them," historian David Wyman argues, "testifies to the fact the world of the late 30s and early 40s was a world without room for the Jews of . . . Europe." The sad saga of the *St. Louis*, which set out from Germany for Cuba in May 1939 with 930 Jewish refugees aboard, was a dramatic case in point. On reaching Havana, the passengers were not allowed to disembark and the ship was turned away. For weeks, as the ship hovered close enough to Miami for the refugees to see the lights of the city, negotiators tried without success to get the U.S. government to provide temporary sanctuary. A telegram to FDR from a committee of the passengers received no reply. The *St. Louis*, memorialized in the movie *Voyage of the Damned*, was forced to sail back to Europe, where many of its passengers eventually died in concentration camps.

Roosevelt was not unsympathetic to the plight of the Jewish refugees. Though anti-Semitism had been part and parcel of the cloistered world in which he and Eleanor had grown up—"The Jew party [was] appalling," Eleanor had written her mother-in-law in 1918 after an evening with Bernard Baruch. "I never wish to hear money, jewels or labels mentioned again" — politics had broadened their attitudes and expanded their sensibilities. During the Roosevelt presidency, though Jews constituted only 3 percent of the U.S. population, they represented nearly 15 percent of Roosevelt's top appointments. Indeed, so prominent were Jews in the Roosevelt administration that bigots routinely referred to the New Deal as the Jew Deal and charged that Roosevelt was himself a Jew. "In the dim distant past," Roosevelt had replied, "[my ancestors] may have been Jews or Catholics or Protestants. What I am interested in is whether they were good citizens and believers in God. I hope they were both."

But it was one thing to sympathize with the plight of the Jewish refugees and quite another to pit his presidency against the xenophobic, anti-Semitic mood of his country in the late 1930s and early '40s. This Roosevelt was unwilling to do. Roper polls confirmed that, though people disapproved of Hitler's treatment of Jews in Germany, the majority of Americans were manifestly unwilling to assist the Jews in practical ways, especially if it meant allowing more Jewish immigration into the U.S. In answer to a question posed in 1938, "What kinds of people do you object to?," Jews were mentioned by 35 percent of the respondents; the next-highest category, at 27 percent, were "noisy, cheap, boisterous and loud people," followed by, "uncultured, unrefined, dumb people" at 14 percent and then all other types. The following year, another Roper poll found that 53 percent of the Americans asked believed Jews were different from everyone else and that these differences should lead to restrictions in business and social life.

The desperate situation of the refugees stranded in Europe was brought to Eleanor's attention on June 24, when she hosted a small dinner at her village apartment for her friend Joe Lash and two members of the European underground, Karl Frank and Joseph Buttinger. Buttinger had been head of the underground socialist movement in Austria while Frank had been organizing in Germany. The question was whether Mrs. Roosevelt could do anything for the leading people of the various socialist parties — German, Austrian, Spanish, and Polish. All these people had fought Hitler for years and were now in mortal danger. Buttinger's group had lists of the people who'd been stranded in France and the ones who had moved on to Spain or Portugal. Could she help?

Agreeing at once that she would do what she could, she rose from the table to put in a call to her husband. But if Eleanor expected public support from her husband at this juncture, she was mistaken. For weeks, ever since the Nazi invasion of the Low Countries, the president had been hearing tales of the great success of the Nazis' various infiltration schemes. In Norway, it was said, thousands of Nazi agents, camouflaged as lecturers, refugees, newspapermen, and diplomatic attachés, had infiltrated the country in the months before the invasion. Then, six weeks before the actual seizure, Norway was flooded with German "tourists" who remained on the scene to help the German troops. In Holland, fifth columnists were said to have figured prominently in the Germans' successful parachute landings, signaling to the planes from the ground and then providing the sky troops with Dutch military and police uniforms when they landed.

Addressing the joint session of Congress on May 16, the president had condemned "the treacherous use of the fifth column by which persons supposed to be peaceful visitors were actually a part of an enemy unit of occupation." Ten days later, in his fireside chat, he had used even more forceful language to warn that "today's threat to our national security is not a matter of military weapons alone. We know of new methods of attack, the Trojan horse, the fifth column that betrays a nation unprepared for treachery. Spies, saboteurs and traitors are all the actors in the new strategy. With all that we must and will deal vigorously."

Thus, while Eleanor and other refugee advocates were fighting to liberalize immigration, Roosevelt was moving in the opposite direction. Preoccupied with the question of subversion, he put the State Department to work on tightening restrictions to prevent infiltration of Nazi agents into the United States. Though it was absurd to believe that Jewish refugees, Hitler's principal victims, would somehow become his principal weapons against the United States, the widespread paranoia about foreigners combined with anti-Semitism to cast a net so wide that everyone except the British children was caught in it.

Eleanor reached Franklin in his study, where he was relaxing with Hopkins at the end of a long workday. "He was somewhat impatient and irritated," Lash recorded in his diary, "that it wasn't taken for granted he was already doing all that was possible. He kept bringing up the difficulties while Mrs. Roosevelt tenaciously kept pointing out the possibilities. 'Congress wouldn't let them in. Quotas are filled. We have tried to get Cuba and other Latin American countries to admit them but so far without success. . . . Can't locate people in France. Spain won't admit even American refugees.' Mrs. Roosevelt interrupted to remind FDR he had always said we could bribe the Spanish and Portuguese governments." There the conversation came to an unsatisfactory end.

When she hung up the phone, Eleanor voiced her inability to understand what had happened to America — the traditional land of asylum, unwilling to admit political refugees. But she said she would take the lists herself and send them to her friend Sumner Welles in the State Department. The European underground should understand it now had a friend at court. In her letter to the State Department the next day, Eleanor said she hoped "the list could be put into the hands of our people in Europe with the request that they do everything they can to protect these refugees. I do not know what Congress will be willing to do, but they might be allowed to come here and be sent to a camp while we are waiting for legislation."

Eleanor's protracted conversation with her husband that evening established the basic pattern their relationship would follow in the years to come. Whereas in the 1930s they had worked side by side in common pursuit of the same goals, now, more and more, she would find herself in the role of the agitator while he remained the politician. On a variety of fronts, she would put pressure on the president when he was tired and would have preferred not to have pressure put upon him. But, as Eleanor's friend Trude Pratt Lash observed, "she had this sense of having to do whatever was humanly possible to do in a difficult time," and nothing, not even her husband, could stop her from trying.

In response to the persistent urging of Eleanor's committee and other refugee groups, the State Department finally agreed to establish a special procedure to expedite the issuance of visitor visas to political, intellectual, and other refugees in special peril in Spain, Portugal, and southern France. Under this procedure, the President's Advisory Committee on Political Refugees (PAC) would take the first crack at evaluating the lists of names, satisfying themselves as to the purpose for which the refugees sought entry and the manner of their departure from the U.S. at the conclusion of the emergency period. Once the list was approved by the PAC, the consuls abroad were supposed to issue the visas automatically.

It was a summer of high hopes. As long as America and other countries were willing to open their doors to the Jews, the Nazis, at this juncture, were still willing to let them go. Liberal use of visitor visas seemed the ideal solution. "I know it is due to your interest," Karl Frank wrote Eleanor the day after the emergency procedure had been put into operation. Already "many hundreds of people have been granted visitors visas."

"We all know," a grateful Joseph Buttinger told Eleanor, "how decisive your protective word was at a time when it looked as if the rescue action would come to a standstill." . . .

Eleanor was in New York on December 2, 1942, for the Day of Mourning and Prayer, sponsored by Jewish leaders to focus public attention on the desperate situation of the European Jews. In various synagogues throughout the city, special services were held; in factories and stores, Jewish laborers halted production for ten minutes, and several radio stations went silent.

The Allied world had been aware for months that Jews from all over Europe were being rounded up and deported by train to various "labor camps" in the East, but a new and devastating report from a reliable source had just reached the United States. The report, from German refugee Gerhart Riegner, revealed that a plan had been discussed in the Führer's headquarters to deport all the Jews in German-occupied countries to concentration camps in the East, where they would be "at one blow exterminated in order to resolve, once and for all the Jewish question in Europe." Though officials in the State Department questioned the validity of the report, it did explain the mass killings in Russia, the round-ups in Holland and France, the crowded trains heading toward Poland.

The next morning, sensitized to the situation by the Day of Prayer, Eleanor noticed a small item buried in the paper which filled her, she said, "with horror." In Poland, it was reported, more than two-thirds of the Jewish population had been massacred. News of massive killings in Poland had been leaking out for months, but this was the first time that Eleanor had fully absorbed the enormity of the slaughter. At the beginning of the year, there was only one camp, Chelmno, to which Jews were being deported and killed; by the end of the year, a half-dozen more, including Auschwitz, Belzec, Treblinka, Sobibor, and Birkenau, were in full operation. In the space of twelve months, nearly three million Polish Jews had been murdered.

The Riegner report so terrified Jewish leader Rabbi Stephen S. Wise that he asked for a meeting with the president. The meeting, which included Adolph Held of the Jewish Labor Committee and Maurice Wertheimer of the American Jewish Congress, took place at noon on December 8. According to Held's notes, the president received the group hospitably and immediately launched into a story of his own about his plans for postwar Germany. When the president had finished, Wise read aloud a two-page statement put together by a group of Jewish leaders which stressed that "unless action is taken immediately the Jews of Hitler's Europe are doomed." The group asked the president to issue a warning against war crimes. He readily agreed, and asked the Jewish leaders to draft a statement for him. The meeting drew to a close. Roosevelt had talked 80 percent of the time. "We shall do all in our power to be of service to your people in this tragic moment," he said as he bid the group goodbye.

But all in his power was not very much. In early November, Roosevelt had requested a new war-powers bill that would have given him the power to suspend laws that were hampering "the free movement of persons, property and information into and out of the United States." The intent of the legislation was simply to make it easier for Allied military and industrial consultants to come in and out of the United States, but had it passed it might have opened the gates of immigration to Jewish refugees. Once this was made clear, the bill had no chance. The powerful conservative coalition, strengthened immeasurably by the by-elections, crushed it. "The ugly truth," *Newsweek* observed, "is that anti-Semitism was a definite factor in the bitter opposition to the President's request." . . .

The midsummer weeks of 1943 witnessed expanding activity in the American Jewish community in behalf of the European Jews. During the last days of July, an Emergency Conference to Save the Jewish People of Europe was convened at the Hotel Commodore in New York City. Through three sweltering days, fifteen hundred people listened to an impressive group of speakers, including Mayor Fiorello LaGuardia, writers

Dorothy Parker and Max Lerner, and former President Herbert Hoover, offer a range of plans for rescue.

Roosevelt's response to a plea for cooperation was a vague, noncommittal message, read at the end of the conference, which spoke of the government's "repeated endeavors" to save the European Jews and promised that "these endeavors will not cease until Nazi power is forever crushed." Yet, far from making repeated endeavors, the government had attempted very little on the rescue front, and the few actions they had taken, such as the two-power American-British Conference on Refugees which had been held in Bermuda the previous spring, had produced little or no results.

Eleanor sent an equally unsatisfactory message to the Emergency Conference, which revealed complete misunderstanding of the situation. Though she was glad "to be of help in any way," she could not figure out, she said, what could be done at the present time. If, however, a program of action could be formulated, she was certain that the American people, "who have been shocked and horrified by the attitude of the Axis powers toward Jewish people will be more than glad to do all they can to alleviate the suffering of these people in Europe and to help them reestablish themselves in other parts of the world if it is possible to evacuate them."

Contrary to Eleanor's assumption, a program of action already existed and was spelled out in detail by the speakers at the conference. The first step, rescue advocates argued, was to form a governmental agency officially charged with rescuing Jews. With this in place, former President Hoover suggested, additional measures could be taken, including Allied protection and support for those Jews who had escaped to neutral countries, pressure on Palestine to absorb more Jews, and preparations for refugee havens in Africa. Beyond these actions, Mayor LaGuardia observed, the U.S. must open its own doors to increased immigration. "Our own government cannot urge other nations to take the initiative before it takes action of its own."

The stumbling block was not ignorance of what should be done but the absence of sustained will and desire on the part of either the government or the people to do anything at all. Despite Eleanor's claim that the American public was "shocked and horrified" about what was going on, the vast majority of ordinary people had only a vague idea of what was happening to the European Jews. Most American newspapers printed very little about the slaughter of the Jews. If mass killings were mentioned, they were generally presented not as the systematic murder of an entire race of people, but as an unfortunate byproduct of the general ravages of war. Nor could most Americans, growing up in a democratic culture, comprehend the unprecedented scale and savagery of Hitler's determination to obliterate the Jews.

Of course, Roosevelt was privy to far greater information than the ordinary citizen. Though neither he nor anyone else in his administration fully understood the extent of what only much later came to be known as the Holocaust, he had read the Riegner report the previous November. He had met that fall with Rabbi Wise and a delegation of Jewish leaders to talk about the slaughter of European Jews. He had spent nearly an hour in July talking with Jan Karski, a leader in the Polish underground who had traveled to London and Washington at great risk to report on the terrible events he had witnessed in Poland. Disguised as a policeman, Karski had seen the insides of the Belzec concentration camp, on the western border of Poland, where thousands of Jews were being gassed. "I am convinced," Karski told Roosevelt, "that there is no exaggeration in the accounts of the plight of the Jews. Our underground authorities are absolutely sure that the Germans are out to exterminate the entire Jewish population of Europe."

Why, then, did Roosevelt fail to provide leadership on this momentous issue? The answer, some suggest, is that he was wholly absorbed in waging a global war and believed that the only solution to the Jewish problem was the final defeat of Hitler and the rooting out of the Nazi system. To the extent that rescue efforts would divert time, attention, and resources from this ultimate goal, thereby lengthening the war, he could not sanction them. Yet, as David Wyman argues in *The Abandonment of the Jews*, "virtually none of the rescue proposals involved enough infringement on the war effort to lengthen the conflict at all or to increase the number of casualties, military or civilian." In fact, when other humanitarian needs were at issue, when refugees in Yugoslavia and Greece were in desperate straits, transportation somehow materialized, the war effort was bent, and the rescue was achieved. Moreover, the rationale that only victory would save the European Jews ignored the chilling question which *The New Republic* asked that summer: "Will any of these Jews survive to celebrate victory?"

The problem lay in the political landscape. Few in Congress showed concern about saving the European Jews. The majority of church leaders were silent on the issue; the intellectual community remained inert. Even the American Jews, who did more than anyone else to publicize the slaughter and press for action, were hampered by a lack of unity. When the Committee for a Jewish Army first proposed the Emergency Conference, rival Jewish leaders and Rabbi Stephen Wise did everything they could to undermine it. Other Jews, like Roosevelt adviser Sam Rosenman, feared that, if too much attention were paid to the plight of the European Jews, American anti-Semitism would increase. Such divisions weakened the pressure on Roosevelt, allowing him to fall back on his rationale that the most important thing he could do to help the Jews was to win the war as quickly as possible.

In mid-August, Peter Bergson, the organizer of the Emergency Conference, met with Eleanor Roosevelt at Hyde Park. Their conversation deepened Eleanor's awareness of the need for action. In her column the next day, she emphasized that the Jews in Europe had suffered as had no other group. "The percentage killed among them," she wrote, "far exceeds the losses among any of the United Nations." Though still admitting that she wasn't sure what could be done to save them, she predicted that "we will be the sufferers if we let great wrongs occur without exerting ourselves to correct them." . . .

An even darker chapter in the history of the world was being written that summer [1944] as Hitler, facing defeat in his conventional war against the Allies, redoubled his efforts to exterminate the Jews. In this phase of the Final Solution, more than one million additional Jews were being rounded up from Western and Central Europe and transported by train to Hitler's "vast kingdom" of secret death camps — Auschwitz, Dachau, Birkenau, Treblinka, Belzec, Chelmno — where nearly two million Jews had already been killed.

In May, the UP reported that three hundred thousand Hungarian Jews were being taken from the Hungarian countryside to Auschwitz and Birkenau. In desperation, rescue advocates pleaded with Washington to bomb the railway lines from Hungary to Auschwitz in order "to slow down or stop the deportations."

The request was forwarded to the newly created War Refugee Board, which the president, under strong pressure from Henry Morgenthau, had finally agreed to establish in January 1944. The goal of the board was "to develop positive, new American programs to aid the victims of Nazism while pressing the Allies and neutrals to take forceful diplomatic action in their behalf." If only it had been set up earlier, War Refugee Board Director John Pehle wistfully noted years later, "things might have been different. Finally there was a place where rescue advocates could go; finally there was a claimant agency mandated to aid the victims of Nazism."

In the early days of spring, the WRB had succeeded in getting Roosevelt to issue his strongest statement yet on the issue, accusing Germany of "the wholesale systematic murder of the Jews" and promising the world that Germany's crimes, "the blackest crimes in all history," would not go unpunished by the Allies. In May, Pehle had scored another victory when Roosevelt agreed to establish an emergency shelter for Jewish refugees in an abandoned army camp in Oswego, New York. Both actions, however, as Pehle freely admits, came far too late to make much difference. If America had lent its prestige to the idea of sanctuaries for refugees in 1939–40, when Hitler was still willing to let the Jews go, perhaps other countries would have followed suit. But once extermination replaced emigration, the only hope for rescue lay in military action aimed at stopping the killing process itself.

The request for Allied bombing of the rail lines ended up on the desk of John McCloy, Stimson's assistant secretary. Though McCloy was not an anti-Semite like Breckinridge Long, he shared some of the stereotypes and prejudices against Jews held by many men of his generation and social milieu, including a suspicion of any information coming from Jewish sources. His answer to the request was a definite no. "The War Department is of the opinion," he wrote, "that the suggested air operation is impracticable," for it would require "diversion of considerable air support" essential for other operations and was of such "doubtful efficacy" that it made no sense.

Pehle refused to give up. The following week, he forwarded another request to McCloy, this time suggesting that the concentration camps themselves should be bombed, so that "in the resultant confusion some of the unfortunate people might be able to escape and hide." Though a large number of inmates would inevitably be killed in such an operation, any action was better than none for a people who were already doomed. What was more, Pehle argued, "if the elaborate murder installations were destroyed, it seems clear the Germans could not reconstruct them for some time."

Once again, McCloy delivered a negative response, arguing that the camps were "beyond the maximum range" of Allied dive-bombers and fighter planes stationed in the U.K., France, and Italy. "The positive solution to this problem," he insisted, repeating the old refrain, "is the earliest possible victory over Germany."

McCloy's argument that the targets were beyond the reach of Allied bombers was not technically true. In fact, long-range American bombers stationed in Italy had flown over Auschwitz several times that spring in search of the I. G. Farben petrochemical plant which was close by. Jan Karski and Elie Wiesel were later given a chance to see some of the aerial reconnaissance photos that were taken on those flights. "It was the saddest thing," Karski recalled. "With a magnifying glass we could actually read the names and numbers of the Hungarian Jews standing on line waiting to be gassed. Yet McCloy claimed the target was too far away." ...

Sorting out Roosevelt's actions and inactions with respect to the European Jews is . . . complicated. He believed that winning the war was the best means of rescuing the Jews. And there was merit to his belief. By the time the news of the systematic murder of the Jews reached the West in mid-942, it was too late to mount a massive rescue effort short of winning the war as quickly as possible. But Roosevelt's intensity of focus blinded him to a series of smaller steps that could have been taken — the War Refugee Board could have been established earlier and given more authority; the United States could have applied more pressure on Germany to release the Jews and more pressure on neutral countries to take them in; the United States Air Force could have bombed the train tracks and the concentration camps. "None of these proposals guaranteed results," holocaust scholar David Wyman admits. "But all deserved serious consideration. . . . Even if few or no lives had been saved, the moral obligation would have been fulfilled."

But in the end, Roosevelt's strengths far outweighed his weaknesses. Despite confusions and conflicts, clashing interests and disparate goals, the American people were successfully combined in an unparalleled national enterprise. Indeed, at times, it seemed as if Roosevelt alone understood the complex and shifting relationship between the nation's effort at home and its struggle across the globe. "More than any other man," historian Eric Larrabee concludes in his study of Roosevelt's wartime leadership, "he ran the war, and ran it well enough to deserve the gratitude of his countrymen then and since, and of those from whom he lifted the yoke of the Axis tyrannies. His conduct as Commander in Chief . . . bears the mark of greatness."

Questions for Discussion

1. Franklin and Eleanor Roosevelt were a remarkably effective political team, even though they led largely separate personal lives. On the issue of helping European Jews during the Second World War, how much of an effect do you think Eleanor had on the President's policy?

2. Goodwin assesses the actions that FDR took to save European Jews. Did he do enough? Could and should he have done more? Do you agree

with the argument that FDR's focus on the overall war effort justified his lack of armed intervention to save more Jews?

3.   What are the factors that a president must consider today when people urge him to intervene in foreign conflicts to prevent mass slaughter or genocide? What kind of leadership role should the United States play, if any, in ethnic conflicts abroad when, unlike in World War II, it may not have compelling and immediate national interests at stake?

10 Truman

DAVID McCULLOUGH

President Harry Truman demonstrated clear-sighted leadership when he made his decision to relieve General Douglas MacArthur of his command during the Korean War. Truman's only miscalculation was estimating the sheer intensity of opinion against the decision—from Congress, the press, the people. But the President stood up to the pressure, and ultimately, historian David McCullough relates, he was vindicated—and the principle of the President as the Commander in Chief was preserved.

IT WAS HARRY TRUMAN'S longstanding conviction that if you did your best in life, did your "damndest" always, then whatever happened you would at least know it was not for lack of trying. But he was a great believer also in the parts played by luck and personality, forces quite beyond effort or determination. And though few presidents had ever worked so hard, or taken their responsibilities so to heart in time of crisis as Truman had since the start of the war in Korea, it was luck, good and bad, and the large influence of personality, that determined the course of events time and again, and never more so than in late December 1950, in the midst of his darkest passage.

Two days before Christmas, on an icy highway north of Seoul, General Walton Walker, commander of the Eighth Army, was killed when his jeep ran head on into an ROK Army truck. Walker's replacement—as requested by MacArthur and approved immediately by Truman—was Matthew Ridgway, who left Washington at once, arriving in Tokyo on Christmas Day. At his meeting with MacArthur the next morning, Ridgway was told to use his own judgment at the front. "The Eighth Army is yours, Matt. Do what you think best." MacArthur, wrote Dean Acheson later, "never uttered wiser words."

That afternoon, Ridgway landed at Taegu, and in the weeks following came a transformation no one had thought possible. Rarely has one individual made so marked a difference in so little time. With what Omar

Bradley called "brilliant, driving, uncompromising leadership," Ridgway restored the fighting spirit of the Eighth Army and turned the tide of war as have few commanders in history.

Since the Chinese onslaught of November 28, the Eighth Army had fallen back nearly 300 miles, to a point just below the 38th parallel, and for a while, Ridgway had no choice but to continue the retreat. Press reports described U.N. forces rolling back down the two main roads through Seoul as a continuous flow morning until night. "The retreating ROK soldiers were the most miserable troops I ever saw," wrote one correspondent. Millions of Korean refugees had also taken to the roads. "What are you going to do when the enemy doesn't care how many men he loses?" an American officer was quoted. Seoul was in flames again. President Rhee and his government had fled to Pusan. Abandoning Seoul, Ridgway withdrew as far as Oswan, near the very point where the first green American troops had gone into action in July. Now, instead of the murderous heat of summer, they fought in murderous cold.

The mood in Washington remained bleak. MacArthur continued to urge a widening of the war—again he proposed bombing and blockading China and utilizing the troops of Chiang Kai-shek—and as before his proposals were rejected. Dire consequences would follow, he implied, unless policy were changed.

> The troops are tired from a long and difficult campaign [MacArthur reported], embittered by the shameful propaganda which has falsely condemned their courage and fighting qualities . . . and their morale will become a serious threat in their battlefield efficiency unless the political basis upon which they are being asked to trade life for time is clearly delineated. . . .

Truman found such messages "deeply disturbing." When a general complained about the morale of his troops, observed George Marshall, the time had come for the general to look to his own morale.

The CIA was advising that it would be "infeasible under existing conditions . . . to hold for a protracted period a position in Korea." The best hope was an armistice. His primary consideration, MacArthur was told, was the safety of his troops and the defense of Japan.

> Under the extraordinary limitations and conditions imposed upon the command in Korea [MacArthur responded] . . . its military position is untenable, but it can hold, if overriding political considerations so dictate, for any length of time up to its complete destruction.

MacArthur called on the administration to recognize the "state of war" imposed by the Chinese, then to drop thirty to fifty atomic bombs on Manchuria and the mainland cities of China.

The Joint Chiefs, too, told Truman that mass destruction of Chinese cities with nuclear weapons was the only way to affect the situation in Korea. But that choice was never seriously considered. Truman simply refused to "go down that trail," in Dean Rusk's words.

> Only once do I recall serious discussion about using nuclear weapons [Rusk later wrote]: when we thought about bombing a large dam on the Yalu River. General Hoyt Vandenberg, Air Force chief of staff, personally had gone to Korea, flown a plane over the dam, and dropped our biggest conventional bomb on it. It made only a little scar on the dams's surface. He returned to Washington and told us that we could knock the dam out only with nuclear weapons. Truman refused.

Truman also still refused to reprimand MacArthur. Rather he treated MacArthur with what Acheson considered "infinite patience" — too much infinite patience, Acheson thought, having by now concluded that the general was "incurably recalcitrant" and fundamentally disloyal to the purposes of his Commander in Chief. On January 13, 1951, Truman sent MacArthur a long, thoughtful telegram, generously praising him for his "splendid leadership" and stressing again the great importance of the whole costly effort in Korea as a means "to demonstrate that aggression will not be accepted by us or by the United Nations." But "great prudence" must be exercised, Truman stated.

> Steps which might in themselves be fully justified and which might lend some assistance to the campaign in Korea would not be beneficial if they thereby involved Japan or Western Europe in large-scale hostilities. . . .
> In the worst case, it would be important that, if we must withdraw from Korea, it be clear to the world that that course is forced upon us by military necessity and that we shall not accept the result politically or militarily until the aggression has been rectified.

Truman had by now declared a national emergency, announced emergency controls on prices and wages, and still greater defense spending — to the amount of $50 billion, more than four times the defense budget at the start of the year. He had put Charles E. Wilson, head of the General Electric Company, in charge of a new Office of Defense Mobilization, appointed General Eisenhower as Supreme Commander of

NATO, and in a radio and television address to the nation on December 15, called on every citizen "to put aside his personal interests for the good of the country." So while doing all he could to avoid a wider war, he was clearly preparing for one.

As General Marshall later attested, "We were at our lowest point."

But then the morning of Wednesday, January 17, Marshall telephoned Truman to read an astonishing report just in from General Joe Collins, who had flown to Korea for talks with Ridgway. "Eighth Army in good shape and improving daily under Ridgway's leadership," Marshall read. "Morale very satisfactory . . . Ridgway confident he can obtain two to three months' delay before having to initiate evacuation. . . . On the whole Eighth Army now in position and prepared to punish severely any mass attack."

Plainly MacArthur's bleak assessment of the situation, his forecasts of doom, had been wrong and the effect of this realization was electrifying. As the word spread through the upper levels of government that day, it would be remembered, one could almost hear the sighs of relief. The long retreat of the Eighth Army — the longest retreat in American military history — had ended. On January 25, 1951, less than a month after Ridgway's arrival, the Eighth Army began "rolling forward," as he said.

Ridgway had gone about his business with drive and common sense, seeing first to the basic needs of his troops — better food, warmer winter clothing, improved Mobile Army Surgical Hospitals (MASH units). He emphasized close communications, less dependence on roads and highways, more attention to holding the high ground, and better, more punishing use of airpower and artillery. With his own confidence, his natural vitality, his frequent and conspicuous presence at the front, dressed for battle with two hand grenades strapped to his chest, he set a strong example. The Army had been Ridgway's life, as it had been for his father before him. He was keenly intelligent, austere, superbly fit at age fifty-six, and already celebrated as the pioneer of the airborne assault in World War II. But Ridgway also understood MacArthur. He admired MacArthur's abilities and knew his limitations. More important, Ridgway both understood and approved of the administration's policy. Not only did he admire Harry Truman, he thought him a great and courageous man.

In Washington, every inclination now, as Bradley would write, was to look "beyond MacArthur" to Ridgway for reliable military judgments. Until now Washington had been almost entirely dependent upon MacArthur's headquarters for information, dependent on MacArthur's own opinions, his strategy. Now all that was over, his influence on planning was ended, a new phase of the war had begun. As far as military operations were concerned, wrote Bradley, MacArthur had become "mainly a prima donna figurehead who had to be tolerated."

With the Eighth Army on the offensive again, advancing relentlessly — to the Han River, to Inchon, then Seoul, retaking what was left of the capital city on March 15 — morale in Washington revived. The advent of the new field commander was, as Acheson said, an event of immeasurable importance. "While General MacArthur was fighting the Pentagon, General Ridgway was fighting the enemy."

With a force of 365,000 men, Ridgway faced an enemy of more than 480,000, but Ridgway's use of concentrated artillery, "the really terrifying strength of our firepower," as he said, plus the spirit of "as fine a fighting field army as our country has yet produced," more than made up for the difference. By the end of March, having inflicted immense casualties on the Chinese, the Eighth Army was again at the 38th parallel.

Yet Ridgway's progress seemed only to distress MacArthur further. The American ambassador in Tokyo, William Sebald, found the Far Eastern Commander "tired and depressed." Unless he was allowed to strike boldly at the enemy, MacArthur said, his dream of a unified Korea was impossible. He complained of a "policy void." He now proposed not only massive attacks on Manchuria, but to "sever" Korea from Manchuria by laying down a field of radioactive wastes, "the by-products of atomic manufacture," all along the Yalu River. As so often before, his request was denied.

MacArthur's need to upstage Ridgway verged on the ridiculous. On the eve of a new Ridgway offensive in late February, MacArthur flew to the front and standing before a dozen correspondents, while Ridgway remained in the background, declared he had "just ordered a resumption of the offensive," when in fact he had had nothing to do with any part of the operation.

Talking to journalists on March 7, MacArthur lamented the "savage slaughter" of Americans inevitable in a war of attrition. When by the middle of March, the tide of battle "began to turn in our favor," as Truman wrote, and Truman's advisers both at the State Department and the Pentagon thought it time to make a direct appeal to China for peace talks, MacArthur refused to respond to inquiries on the subject. Instead he decried any "further military restrictions" on his command.

To MacArthur, as he later wrote, it appeared that Truman's nerves were at a breaking point — "not only his nerves, but what was far more menacing in the Chief Executive of a country at war — his nerve."

Truman ordered careful preparation of a cease-fire proposal. On March 21, the draft of a presidential statement was submitted for approval to the other seventeen U.N. nations with troops serving in Korea. On March 20 the Chiefs of Staff had informed MacArthur of what was happening — sending him what Truman called the "meat paragraphs" of the statement in a message that seems to have impressed MacArthur as nothing else had that there was indeed to be no all-out war with Red China. His response so jarred Washington as to leave a number of people wondering if perhaps he had lost his mind — first there had been Forrestal, then Louis Johnson, now MacArthur. Years afterward Bradley would speculate that possibly MacArthur's realization that his war on China was not to be "snapped his brilliant but brittle mind."

On the morning of Saturday, March 24, in Korea (Friday the 23rd in Washington), MacArthur, without warning, tried to seize the initiative in a manner calculated only to inflame the situation. He issued his own florid proclamation to the Chinese Communists, which in effect was an ultimatum. He began by taunting the Red Chinese for their lack of industrial power, their poor military showing in Korea against a U.N. force restricted by "inhibitions." More seriously, MacArthur threatened to expand the war.

> The enemy, therefore, must by now be painfully aware that a decision of the United States to depart from its tolerant effort to contain the war to the areas of Korea, through an expansion of our military operations to his coastal areas and interior bases, would doom Red China to the risk of imminent military collapse.

In conclusion, MacArthur said he personally "stood ready at any time" to meet with the Chinese commander to reach a settlement.

All Truman's careful preparations of a cease-fire proposal were now in vain. MacArthur had cut the ground out from under him. Later MacArthur would dismiss what he had said as a "routine communiqué." Yet his own devoted aide, General Courtney Whitney, would describe it as a bold effort to stop one of the most disgraceful plots in American history, meaning the administration's plan to appease China.

The news reached Washington after nightfall.

MacArthur, with his "pronunciamento," wrote Acheson, had perpetrated a major act of sabotage. To Acheson, it was "insubordination of the grossest sort"; to Bradley, an "unforgivable and irretrievable act."

At eleven o'clock that night in Washington, Friday, March 23, Acheson, Lovett, Rusk, and two other senior State Department officials, Alexis Johnson and Lucius Battle, met at Acheson's house in Georgetown and talked until past midnight. Lovett, ordinarily a man of imperturbable temperament, was angriest of all. MacArthur, he said, must be removed at once. Acheson agreed and quoted Euripides: "Whom the gods would destroy they first make mad."

At Blair House, Truman sat in an upstairs study reading and rereading the text of the MacArthur ultimatum. "I couldn't send a message to the Chinese after that," he would say in later years, trying to recall the disappointment and fury he felt. "I was ready to kick him into the North China Sea . . . I was never so put out in my life. . . . MacArthur thought he was the proconsul for the government of the United States and could do as he damned pleased."

In his *Memoirs*, Truman would write that he now knew what he must do about MacArthur.

> This was a most extraordinary statement for a military commander of the United Nations to issue on his own responsibility. It was an act totally disregarding all directives to abstain from any declarations on foreign policy. It was in open defiance of my orders as President and as Commander in Chief. This was a challenge to the President under the Constitution. It also flouted the policy of the United Nations. . . .
>
> By this act MacArthur left me no choice—I could no longer tolerate his insubordination. . . .

At the end of a routine morning staff meeting, the President quietly announced—"So you won't have to read about it in the papers"—that he had decided to fire General MacArthur. He was sure, Truman added, that MacArthur had wanted to be fired.

He was sure also that he himself faced a political storm, "a great furor," unlike any in his political career. From beyond the office windows, the noise of construction going on in the White House was so great that several of the staff had to strain to hear what he was saying.

At 3:15 that afternoon, Acheson, Marshall, Bradley, and Harriman reported to the Oval office, bringing the drafted orders. Truman looked them over, borrowed a fountain pen from Bill Hassett, and signed his name.

General MacArthur learned of his recall while at lunch in Tokyo, when his wife handed him a brown Signal Corps envelope.

If Truman had only let him know how he felt, MacArthur would say privately a few hours later, he would have retired "without difficulty." Where the *Tribune* reporter got his tip was never learned. MacArthur would later testify that he had never given any thought to resigning.

According to what MacArthur had been told by an unnamed but "eminent" medical authority, Truman's "mental instability" was the result of malignant hypertension, "characterized by bewilderment and confusion of thought." Truman, MacArthur predicted, would be dead in six months.

TRUMAN FIRES MACARTHUR

The headline across the early edition of the Washington *Post*, April 11, 1951, was the headline everywhere in the country and throughout much of the world, with only minor variations. The reaction was stupendous, the outcry from the American people shattering. Truman had known he would have to face a storm, but however dark his premonitions, he could not possibly have measured what was coming. No one did, no one could have. One southern senator in the course of the day described the people in his part of the country as "almost hysterical." The senator himself was almost hysterical. So were scores of others on Capitol Hill and millions of Americans.

The day on Capitol Hill was described as "one of the bitterest . . . in modern times." Prominent Republicans, including Senator Taft, spoke angrily of impeaching the President. The full Republican leadership held an angry emergency meeting in Joe Martin's office at 9:30 in the morning, after which Martin talked to reporters of "impeachments," the accent on the plural. "We might want the impeachments of 1 or 50." A full-dress congressional investigation of the President's war policy was in order. General MacArthur, announced Martin, would be invited to air his views before a joint session of Congress.

Senator Nixon demanded MacArthur's immediate reinstatement. Senator Jenner declared the country was "in the hands of a secret coterie" directed by Russian spies. When, on the floor of the Senate, Jenner shouted, "Our only choice is to impeach President Truman and find out who is the secret invisible government which has so cleverly led our country down the road to destruction," the gallery broke into applause.

A freshman Democrat from Oklahoma, Senator Robert Kerr, rose to defend the President. If the Republicans believed the nation's security depended on following the policy of General MacArthur, Kerr said, then they should call for a declaration of war against Red China. Otherwise, Republican support of MacArthur was a mockery. Tom Connally reminded his colleagues that Americans had always insisted on civilian control over the military, and three Senate Republicans, Duff of Pennsylvania, Saltonstall and Lodge of Massachusetts, spoke in agreement.

But such voices were lost in a tempest of Republican outrage. The general's dismissal was "another Pearl Harbor," a "great day for the Russian Communists." MacArthur had been fired "because he told the truth." "God help the United States," said Senator James P. Kem, Republican of Missouri.

In New York two thousand longshoremen walked off their jobs in protest over the firing of MacArthur. A Baltimore women's group announced plans for a march on Washington in support of the general. Elsewhere enraged patriots flew flags at half-staff, or upside down. People signed petitions, fired off furious letters and telegrams to Washington. In Worcester, Massachusetts, and San Gabriel, California, Truman was burned in effigy. In Houston, a Protestant minister became so angry dictating a telegram to the White House that he died of a heart attack.

The legislatures of four states — Florida, Michigan, Illinois, and California — voted resolutions condemning the President's action, while the Los Angeles City Council adjourned for a day of "sorrowful contemplation of the political assassination of General MacArthur." In Chicago, in a frontpage editorial, the *Tribune* called for immediate impeachment proceedings:

> President Truman must be impeached and convicted. His hasty and vindictive removal of Gen. MacArthur is the culmination of a series of acts which have shown that he is unfit, morally and mentally, for his high office. . . . The American nation has never been in a greater danger. It is led by a fool who is surrounded by knaves. . . .

"IMPEACH THE IMBECILE" . . . "IMPEACH THE LITTLE WARD POLITICIAN STUPIDITY FROM KANSAS CITY" . . . "SUGGEST YOU LOOK FOR ANOTHER HISS IN BLAIR HOUSE," read telegrams typical of those pouring into Washington. In the hallways of the Senate and House office buildings, Western Union messengers made their deliveries with bushel baskets. According to one tally, of the 44,358 telegrams received by Republicans in Congress during the first 48 hours following Truman's announcement, all but 334 condemned him or took the side of MacArthur, and the majority called for Truman's immediate removal from office.

Republicans were overjoyed. "This is the biggest windfall that has ever come to the Republican Party," exclaimed Senator Styles Bridges.

A number of prominent liberals — Eleanor Roosevelt, Walter Reuther, Justice William O. Douglas — publicly supported Truman. Douglas, who had told Truman as early as October that MacArthur should be fired, wrote, "In the days ahead you may need the strength of all your friends. This note is to let you know that I am and will be in your corner . . . I know you are right."

While by far the greatest clamor came from those in the country outraged over what Truman had done, there was no lack of conviction, even passion, among people who felt he was in the right, that a fundamental principle was at stake. And to many of these same people, how one felt about Harry Truman personally was immaterial.

"It makes not the slightest difference if Mr. Harry Truman is an ignorant person who never graduated from college, who once worked in a haberdashery shop, who was a protégé of one of our worst city bosses and came into the presidency through accident," the Reverend Dr. Duncan E. Littlefield said in a sermon at the Fountain Street Baptist Church in Grand Rapids, Michigan.

> Neither does it make any difference if General MacArthur is a man of astounding personality, tremendous achievement, graduated first in his class in the great College of the Army and has had a distinguished career and has proven a wonderful administrator of the Japanese people or that we like him better than we do Harry S. Truman. Principle, *principle*, must always be above personality and it must be above expediency. The principle here we recognize . . . [is] that control of this country must come through the president and the departments that are organized under him and through Congress, and that any decision that comes from that person through those means is not to be dismissed because we don't like the personality who expressed it, nor is it to be overridden because we have a conquering hero. . . .

Another letter of support addressed to the President came from the Washington *Post* music critic, Paul Hume.

Throughout Europe, MacArthur's dismissal was greeted as welcome news. "MAC IS SACKED," declared the London *Evening Standard*. The French, reported Janet Flanner in *The New Yorker*, were "solidly for Truman." Not a single paper in Paris had failed to support his decision.

But most impressive was the weight of editorial opinion at home, despite vehement assaults in the McCormick, Hearst, and Scripps-Howard newspapers, or the renewed glorification of MacArthur in Henry Luce's *Time* and *Life*.

The Washington *Post*, The *New York Times,* the New York *Post*, the Baltimore *Sun*, the Atlanta *Journal*, the Miami *Daily News*, the Boston *Globe*, the Chicago *Sun-Times*, the Milwaukee *Journal*, the St. Louis *Post-Dispatch*, the Denver *Post*, the Seattle *Times*, the *Christian Science Monitor*, all these and more endorsed Truman's decision. Importantly the list also included such staunch Republican papers as the Des Moines *Register and Tribune* and the New York *Herald-Tribune*, which went out of its way to praise Truman as well for his strength of character:

The most obvious fact about the dismissal of General MacArthur is that he virtually forced his own removal. In high policy as in war there is no room for a divided command. . . . General MacArthur is a soldier of the highest abilities . . . to lose his service and his talents is in a very true sense a tragedy for the nation, yet he is the architect of a situation which really left the President with no other course. With one of those strokes of boldness and decision which are characteristic of Mr. Truman in emergencies, a very difficult and dangerous problem has been met in the only way it could have been met. . . .

In his "Today and Tomorrow" column, Walter Lippman commended Truman and Marshall both for having "done their duty." And the working press, according to the *Saturday Review*, privately sided with Truman by a margin of six to one, though most reporters thought the dismissal had been poorly handled.

The clamor in the country, the outrage, the noisy hostility to Truman, the adulation of MacArthur continued, however, and would grow greater still when MacArthur made his triumphal return. Nothing had so stirred the political passions of the country since the Civil War.

At the heart of the tumult was anger and frustration over the war in Korea. Nobody liked it. Senator Wherry had begun calling it "Truman's War," and the name caught on. People were sick of Truman's War, frustrated and a bit baffled by talk of a "limited war." America didn't fight to achieve a stalemate, and the cost in blood had become appalling. If it was a United Nations effort, then the United States seemed to be bearing the heavy side of the burden. According to the latest figures, there were more than ten thousand Americans dead, another fifty thousand wounded or missing in action. The country wanted it over. MacArthur at least offered victory.

To a great part of the country MacArthur was a glorious figure, a real life, proven American hero, the brilliant, handsome general who had led American forces to stunning triumph in the greatest of all wars wherein there had never been any objective but complete and total victory. "Douglas MacArthur was the personification of the big man . . . Harry Truman was almost a professional little man," wrote *Time* in a considerably less than unbiased attempt to appraise the national mood, but one that nonetheless applied to a large part of the populace. For someone of Truman's modest attainments, a man of his "stature," to have fired Douglas MacArthur seemed to many Americans an act smacking of insolence and vindictiveness, not to say dreadful judgment. Nor did the way it happened seem right. Reportedly, the firing had been carefully timed so as to make the morning papers "and catch the Republicans in bed." Rumors also attributed the announcement to another of Truman's dead-of-the-night temper tantrums, or heavy drinking. In a speech in Milwaukee having called Truman a "son-of-a-bitch," Joe McCarthy charged that the decision had been influenced by "bourbon and Benedictine." Even to more fairminded Republicans than McCarthy and others of the party's vociferous right wing — as to a great many Democrats — it seemed to have been a graceless, needlessly unkind way to terminate a great career. Who did "little Harry Truman" think he was?

Old admirers of Franklin Roosevelt speculated on how differently "the master politician" might have handled things — made MacArthur ambassador to the Court of St. James's, perhaps.

But in a larger way, for many, the firing of MacArthur was yet another of those traumatic turns of events of recent years — like the fall of China to Communist control, like the advent of the Russian bomb — that seemed to signal a world out of joint, a world increasingly hard to understand and threatening.

According to a Gallup Poll, 69 percent of the country backed General MacArthur. The fact that the country and nearly every leading Republican had strongly supported Truman's decision to go into Korea the previous June, the fact that in November MacArthur, the supreme military strategist, had presided over one of the worst debacles in American military history, or that only 30 percent of the country expressed a willingness to go to war with China, were all overlooked.

Truman was not to appear at a big public event until April 20 — not until after MacArthur had made his return and appeared before Congress — and when he did, to throw out the first ball at the opening game at Griffith Stadium, he was booed to his face, something that had not happened since Herbert Hoover attended a ball game in 1931.

Except for a brief broadcast from the White House the night following his dismissal of MacArthur, April 11, Truman had maintained silence on the matter. General MacArthur was "one of our greatest military commanders," he told the nation, but the cause of world peace was far more important than any single individual.

> The change in commands in the Far East means no change whatever in the policy of the United States. We will carry on the fight in Korea with vigor and determination. . . . The new commander, Lieutenant General Matthew Ridgway, has already demonstrated that he has the great qualities of military leadership needed for this task.
>
> We are ready, at any time, to negotiate for a restoration of peace

in the area. But we will not engage in appeasement. We are only interested in real peace. . . .

We do not want to widen the conflict. . . .

He went about his schedule as though all were normal. On April 13, he had his picture taken as, smiling confidently, he began his seventh year in the Oval Office. One evening he and Bess went to the theater, another to see a British film of Offenbach's *Tales of Hoffman*.

MacArthur landed at San Francisco Tuesday, April 17, to a delirious reception. He had been away from the country for fourteen years. Until now, the American people had had no chance to see and cheer him, to welcome the hero home. Ten thousand were at the San Francisco airport. So great were the crowds on the way into the city, it took two hours for the motorcade to reach his hotel. "The only politics I have," MacArthur told a cheering throng, "is contained in a simple phrase known to all of you — God Bless America."

When Truman met with reporters the next day, April 18, at his first press conference since the start of the crisis, he dashed all their expectations by refusing to say anything on the subject. Scheduled to appear before the American Society of Newspaper Editors on Thursday, April 19, the day MacArthur was to go before Congress, Truman canceled his speech, because he felt it should be the general's day and did not wish anything to detract from it.

Only in a few personal letters did Truman touch on the matter, and then briefly, simply, and without apologies or complicated explanations. "I was sorry to have to reach a parting of the way with the big man in Asia," he wrote to Eisenhower, "but he asked for it and I had to give it to him."

There would be "hell to pay" for it for perhaps six or seven weeks, he told his staff and the Cabinet. But eventually people would come to their senses, including more and more Republican politicians who would grow doubtful of all-out support for the general. Given some time, MacArthur would be reduced to human proportions. Meanwhile, Truman could withstand the bombardment, for in the long run, he knew, he would be judged to have made the right decision. He had absolutely no doubt of that. "The American people will come to understand that what I did had to be done." . . .

At 12:31 P.M., Thursday, April 19, in a flood of television lights, Douglas MacArthur walked down the same aisle in the House of Representatives as had Harry Truman so often since 1945, and the wild ovation from the packed chamber, the intense, authentic drama of the moment, were such as few had ever beheld.

Neither the President's Cabinet, nor the Supreme Court, nor any of the Joint Chiefs were present.

Wearing a short "Eisenhower" jacket, without decoration, the silvery circles of five-star rank glittering on his shoulders, MacArthur paused to shake hands with Vice President Barkley, then stepped to the rostrum, his face "an unreadable mask." Only after complete silence had fallen did he begin.

"I address you with neither rancor nor bitterness in the fading twilight of life, with but one purpose in mind: to serve my country."

There was ringing applause and the low, vibrant voice continued, the speaker in full command of the moment.

The decision to intervene in support of the Republic of Korea had been sound from a military standpoint, MacArthur affirmed. But when he had called for reinforcements, he was told they were not available. He had "made clear," he said, that if not permitted to destroy the enemy bases north of the Yalu, if not permitted to utilize the 800,000 Chinese troops on Formosa, if not permitted to blockade the China coast, then "the position of the command from a military standpoint forbade victory. . . . " And war's "very object" was victory. How could it be otherwise? "In war, indeed," he said, repeating his favorite slogan, "there can be no substitute for victory. There were some who, for varying reasons, would appease Red China. They were blind to history's clear lesson, for history teaches, with unmistakable emphasis, that appeasement begets new and bloodier war."

He was provocative, and defiant. Resounding applause or cheers followed again and again — thirty times in thirty-four minutes. He said nothing of bombing China's industrial centers, as he had proposed. And though he said "every available means" should be applied to bring victory, he made no mention of his wish to use atomic bombs, or to lay down a belt of radioactivity along the Yalu. He had been severely criticized for his views, he said. Yet, he asserted, his views were "fully shared" by the Joint Chiefs — a claim that was altogether untrue and that brought a deafening ovation. Republicans and most spectators in the galleries leaped to their feet, cheering and stamping. It was nearly a minute before he could begin again.

To those who said American military strength was inadequate to face the enemy on more than one front, MacArthur said he could imagine no greater expression of defeatism. "You cannot appease or otherwise surrender to Communism in Asia without simultaneously undermining our efforts to halt its advance in Europe." To confine the war to Chinese aggression in Korea only was to follow a path of "prolonged indecision."

"Why, my soldiers asked of me, surrender military advantages to an enemy in the field?" He paused, then, softly, his voice almost a whisper, he said, "I could not answer."

A record 30 million people were watching on television and the performance was masterful. The use of the rich voice, the timing, surpassed that of most actors. The oratorical style was of a kind not heard in Congress in a very long time. It recalled, as one television critic wrote, "a yesteryear of the theater," and it held the greater part of the huge audience wholly enraptured. Work had stopped in offices and plants across the country, so people could watch. Saloons and bars were jammed. Schoolchildren saw the "historic hour" in classrooms or were herded into assemblies or dining halls to listen by radio. Whether they had any idea what the excitement was about, they knew it was "important."

"When I joined the Army, even before the turn of the century, it was the fulfillment of all my boyish hopes and dreams," MacArthur said, his voice dropping as he began the famous last lines, the stirring, sentimental, ambiguous peroration that the speech would be remembered for.

> The hopes and dreams have long since vanished. But I still remember the refrain of one of the most popular barracks ballads of that day which proclaimed most proudly that, "Old soldiers never die. They just fade away." And like the old soldier of the ballad, I now close my military career and just fade away—an old soldier who tried to do his duty as God gave him the light to see that duty.
> Goodbye.

A "hurricane of emotion" swept the room. Hands reached out to him. Many in the audience were weeping. "We heard God speak here today, God in the flesh, the voice of God!" exclaimed Republican Representative Dewey Short of Missouri, a former preacher. To Joe Martin, it was "the climaxing" of the most emotional moment he had known in thirty-five years in Congress. Theatrics were a part of the congressional way of life, Martin knew, but nothing had ever equaled this.

It was MacArthur's finest hour, and the crescendo of public adulation that followed, beginning with a triumphal parade through Washington that afternoon, and climaxing the next day in New York with a thunderous ticker-tape parade, was unprecedented in American history. Reportedly 7,500,000 people turned out in New York, more than had welcomed

Eisenhower in 1945, more even than at the almost legendary welcome for Lindbergh in 1927. It was "awesome," wrote *Time*. "Everybody cheered . . . a man of chin-out affirmation, who seemed a welcome contrast to men of indecision and negation."

But, in fact, not everybody cheered. There were places along the parade route in New York where, as MacArthur's open car passed, people stood silently, just watching and looking, anything but pleased. In Washington, one senator had confided to a reporter that he had never feared more for his country than during MacArthur's speech. "I honestly felt that if the speech had gone on much longer there might have been a march on the White House." Even *Time* noted that while Republicans in Congress might consider MacArthur a godsend, few were ready to endorse his proposals.

Truman had not listened to MacArthur's speech, or watched on television. He had spent the time at his desk in the Oval Office, meeting with Dean Acheson as usual at that hour on Thursdays, after which he went back to Blair House for lunch and a nap. At some point, however, he did read what MacArthur had said. Speaking privately, he remarked that he thought it "a bunch of damn bullshit."

As Truman had anticipated, the tumult began to subside. For seven weeks in the late spring of 1951, the Senate Foreign Relations and Armed Services committees held joint hearings to investigate MacArthur's dismissal. Chaired by Democratic Senator Richard B. Russell, the inquiry opened on May 3 in the same marble Caucus Room, 318 of the Senate Office Building, where the Truman Committee had conducted its sessions. Though the hearings were closed, authorized transcripts of each day's sessions, edited for military security reasons, were released hourly to the press.

MacArthur, the first witness, testified for three days, arguing that his way in Korea was the way to victory and an end to the slaughter. He had seen as much blood and disaster as any man alive, he told the senators, but never such devastation as during his last time in Korea. "After I looked at that wreckage and those thousands of women and children and everything, I vomited. Now are you going to let that go on . . . ?" The politicians in Washington had introduced a "new concept into military operations—the concept of appeasement," its purpose only "to go on indefinitely . . . indecisively, fighting with no mission. . . . "

But he also began to sound self-absorbed and oddly disinterested in global issues. He would admit to no mistakes, no errors of judgment. Failure to anticipate the size of the Chinese invasion, for example, had been the fault of the CIA. Any operation he commanded was crucial, other considerations were always of less importance. Certain that his strategy of war on China would not bring in the Soviets, he belittled the danger of a larger conflict. But what if he happened to be wrong, he was asked. What if another world war resulted? That, said MacArthur, was not his responsibility. "My responsibilities were in the Pacific, and the Joint Chiefs of Staff and various agencies of the Government are working night and day for an over-all solution to the global problem. Now I am not familiar with their studies. I haven't gone into it. . . ." To many, it seemed he had made the President's case.

The great turning point came with the testimony of Marshall, Bradley, and the Joint Chiefs, who refuted absolutely MacArthur's claim that they agreed with his strategy. Truman, from the start of the crisis, had known he needed the full support of his military advisers before declaring his decision on MacArthur. Now it was that full support, through nineteen days of testimony, that not only gave weight and validity to the decision, but discredited MacArthur in a way nothing else could have.

Speaking solemnly, Marshall began by saying it was "a very distressing necessity, a very distressing occasion that compels me to appear here this morning and in effect in almost direct opposition to a great many views and actions of General MacArthur. He is a brother Army officer, a man for whom I have tremendous respect. . . ."

The administration was not turning its back on an easy victory in Korea, Marshall said, because there could be no easy or decisive victory in Korea short of another world war. The present policy might indeed seem costly, but not compared to an atomic war. There had been complaints of stalemate, demands for quick, decisive solutions at the time of the Berlin crisis, too, he reminded the senators. The war in Korea was in its tenth month, but the Berlin crisis had lasted almost fifteen months before ending in a "notable victory."

Just what did Secretary Marshall consider the "Korean business," he was asked. "A police action? A large or small war? . . ."

"I would characterize it as a limited war which I hope will remain limited," Marshall replied evenly.

Bradley, his first day in the witness chair, testified with unexpected vigor and delivered a telling blow with what would be the most quoted line of the hearings. MacArthur's program to step up and widen the war with China, Bradley said, would "involve us in the wrong war, at the wrong place, at the wrong time, and with the wrong enemy."

Never, said the Joint Chiefs, had they subscribed to MacArthur's plan for victory, however greatly they admired him.

From a purely military standpoint, General Collins was asked, had

General MacArthur's conduct of the war in Korea been compatible with General MacArthur's outstanding conduct of the war in the Pacific from 1941 to 1945? That, said Collins, was a question he would prefer not to answer, and no one insisted.

The dismissal of MacArthur, said all of them — Marshall, Bradley, the Joint Chiefs — was more than warranted, it was a necessity. Given the circumstances, given the seriousness of MacArthur's opposition to the policy of the President, his challenge to presidential authority, said Marshall, there had been "no other course but to relieve him."

The fidelity of the military high command to the principle of civilian control of the military was total and unequivocal.

Such unanimity of opinion on the part of the country's foremost and most respected military leaders seemed to leave Republican senators stunned. As James Reston wrote in *The New York Times*, "MacArthur, who had started as the prosecutor, had now become the defendant."

The hearings ground on and grew increasingly dull. The MacArthur hysteria was over, interest waned. When in June, MacArthur set off on a speaking tour through Texas, insisting he had no presidential ambitions, he began to sound more and more shrill and vindictive, less and less like a hero. He attacked Truman, appeasement, high taxes, and "insidious forces working from within." His crowds grew steadily smaller. Nationwide, the polls showed a sharp decline in his popular appeal. The old soldier was truly beginning to fade away. . . .

Truman would regard the decision as among the most important he made as President. He did not, however, agree with those who said it had shown what great courage he had. (Harriman, among others, would later speak of it as one of the most courageous steps ever taken by any President.) "Courage didn't have anything to do with it," Truman would say emphatically. "General MacArthur was insubordinate and I fired him. That's all there was to it."

But if the firing of MacArthur had taken a heavy toll politically, if Truman as President had been less than a master of persuasion, he had accomplished a very great deal and demonstrated extraordinary patience and strength of character in how he rode out the storm. His policy in Korea — his determined effort to keep the conflict in bounds — had not been scuttled, however great the aura of the hero-general, or his powers as a spellbinder. The principle of civilian control over the military, challenged as never before in the nation's history, had survived, and stronger than ever. The President had made his point and, with the backing of his generals, he had made it stick.

Questions for Discussion

1.   Which actions of General MacArthur were inappropriate and violated the principle of civilian control over the military? What should MacArthur have done differently in expressing his doubts about President Truman's policies in Korea? Did Truman actually wait longer than necessary in making his decision to fire MacArthur?

2.   President Truman stated that his firing of General MacArthur did not really require courage, because the case was so clear and Truman knew he was right. Do you think this assessment is accurate, or is Truman being too modest? What do you think the most difficult aspect of the firing was for Truman in the months afterward?

3.   Are you surprised that all of the Joint Chiefs of Staff and other military figures who testified before Congress endorsed Truman's firing of MacArthur? Do you believe that today's military brass is any more "political" than during the 1950s, and do you think that these officers would stand uniformly behind a president in a similar situation?

11 The Triumph of Watergate

WALTER KARP

VANCE BOURJAILY

This selection recounts step-by-step the events that culminated with the resignation of the 37th President, Richard M. Nixon. The Watergate Scandal remains today an unfortunate monument to disastrous decision making based on the questionable ethics of a powerful but insular administration that believed it was beyond reproach. We can look back at it as another major challenge, though not the last, to the durability of the Founders' vision for government.

[IN] AUGUST, [1974], the thirty-seventh President of the United States, facing imminent impeachment, resigned his high office and passed out of our lives. "The system worked," the nation exclaimed, heaving a sigh of relief. What had brought that relief was the happy extinction of the prolonged fear that the "system" might not work at all. But what was it that had inspired such fears? When I asked myself that question recently, I found I could scarcely remember. Although I had followed the Watergate crisis with minute attention, it had grown vague and formless in my mind, like a nightmare recollected in sunshine. It was not until I began working my way through back copies of the *New York Times* that I was able to remember clearly why I used to read my morning paper with forebodings for the country's future.

The Watergate crisis had begun in June 1972 as a "third-rate burglary" of the Democratic National Committee headquarters in Washington's Watergate building complex. By late March 1973 the burglary and subsequent efforts to obstruct its investigation had been laid at the door of the White House. By late June, Americans were asking themselves whether their President had or had not ordered the payment of "hush money" to silence a Watergate burglar. Investigated by a special Senate committee headed by Sam Ervin of North Carolina, the scandal continued to deepen and ramify during the summer of 1973. By March 1974 the third-rate burglary of 1972 had grown into an unprecedented constitutional crisis.

By then it was clear beyond doubt that President Richard M. Nixon stood at the center of a junto of henchmen without parallel in our history. One of Nixon's attorneys general, John Mitchell, was indicted for obstructing justice in Washington and for impeding a Securities and Exchange Commission investigation in New York. Another, Richard Kleindienst, had criminally misled the Senate Judiciary Committee in the President's interest. The acting director of the Federal Bureau of Investigation, L. Patrick Gray, had burned incriminating White House documents at the behest of a presidential aide. Bob Haldeman, the President's chief of staff, John Ehrlichman, the President's chief domestic adviser, and Charles Colson, the President's special counsel, all had been indicted for obstructing justice in the investigation of the Watergate burglary. John Dean, the President's legal counsel and chief accuser, had already pleaded guilty to the same charge. Dwight Chapin, the President's appointments secretary, faced trial for lying to a grand jury about political sabotage carried out during the 1972 elections. Ehrlichman and two other White House aides were under indictment for conspiring to break into a psychiatrist's office and steal confidential information about one of his former patients, Daniel Ellsberg. By March 1974 some twenty-eight presidential aides or election officials had been indicted for crimes carried out in the President's interest. Never before in American history had a President so signally failed to fulfill his constitutional duty to "take care that the laws be faithfully executed."

It also had been clear for many months that the thirty-seventh President of the United States did not feel bound by his constitutional duties. He insisted that the requirements of national security as he and he alone saw fit to define it, released him from the most fundamental legal and constitutional constraints. In the name of "national security," the President had created a secret band of private detectives, paid with private funds, to carry out political espionage at the urging of the White House. In the name of "national security," the President had approved the warrantless wiretapping of news reporters. In the name of "national security," he had approved a secret plan for massive, illegal surveillance of American citizens. He had encouraged his aides' efforts to use the Internal Revenue Service to harass political "enemies" — prominent Americans who endangered "national security" by publicly criticizing the President's Vietnam War policies.

The framers of the Constitution had provided one and only one remedy for such lawless abuse of power: impeachment in the House of Representatives and trial in the Senate for "high Crimes and Misdemeanors." There was absolutely no alternative. If Congress had not held President Nixon accountable for lawless conduct of his office, then Congress would have condoned a lawless Presidency. If Congress had not struck from the President's hands the despot's cudgel of "national security," then Congress would have condoned a despotic Presidency.

Looking through the back issues of the *New York Times*, I recollected in a flood of ten-year-old memories what it was that had filled me with such foreboding. It was the reluctance of Congress to act. I felt anew my fury when members of Congress pretended that nobody really cared about Watergate except the "media" and the "Nixon-haters." The real folks "back home," they said, cared only about inflation and the gasoline shortage. I remembered the exasperating actions of leading Democrats, such as a certain Senate leader who went around telling the country that President Nixon could not be impeached because in America a person was presumed innocent until proven guilty. Surely the senator knew that impeachment was not a verdict of guilt but a formal accusation made in the House leading to trial in the Senate. Why was he muddying the waters, I wondered, if not to protect the President? It had taken one of the most outrageous episodes in the history of the Presidency to compel Congress to make even a pretense of action.

Back on July 16, 1973, a former White House aide named Alexander Butterfield had told the Ervin committee that President Nixon secretly tape-recorded his most intimate political conversations. On two solemn occasions that spring the President had sworn to the American people that he knew nothing of the Watergate cover-up until his counsel John Dean had told him about it on March 21, 1973. From that day forward, Nixon had said, "I began intensive new inquiries into this whole matter." Now we learned that the President had kept evidence secret that would exonerate him completely — if he were telling the truth. Worse yet, he wanted it kept secret. Before Butterfield had revealed the existence of the tapes, the President had grandly announced that "executive privilege will not be invoked as to any testimony [by my aides] concerning possible criminal conduct, in the matters under investigation. I want the public to learn the truth about Watergate. . . ."After the existence of the tapes was revealed, however, the President showed the most ferocious resistance to disclosing the "truth about Watergate." He now claimed that executive privilege — hitherto a somewhat shadowy presidential prerogative — gave a President "absolute power" to withhold any taped conversation he chose, even those urgently needed in the ongoing criminal investigation then being conducted by a special Watergate prosecutor. Nixon even claimed, through his lawyers, that the judicial branch of the federal government was "absolutely without power to reweigh that choice or to make a different resolution of it."

In the U.S. Court of Appeals the special prosecutor, a Harvard Law School professor named Archibald Cox, called the President's claim "intolerable." Millions of Americans found it infuriating. The court found it groundless. On October 12, 1973, it ordered the President to surrender nine taped conversations that Cox had been fighting to obtain for nearly three months.

Determined to evade the court order, the President on October 19 announced that he had devised a "compromise." Instead of handing over the recorded conversations to the court, he would submit only edited summaries. To verify their truthfulness, the President would allow Sen. John Stennis of Mississippi to listen to the tapes. As an independent verifier, the elderly senator was distinguished by his devotion to the President's own overblown conception of a "strong" Presidency. When Nixon had ordered the secret bombing of Cambodia, he had vouchsafed the fact to Senator Stennis, who thought that concealing the President's secret war from his fellow senators was a higher duty than preserving the Senate's constitutional role in the formation of United States foreign policy.

On Saturday afternoon, October 20, I and millions of other Americans sat by our television sets while the special prosecutor explained why he could not accept "what seems to me to be non-compliance with the court's order." Then the President flashed the dagger sheathed within his "compromise." At 8:31 P.M. television viewers across the country learned that he had fired the special prosecutor; that attorney general Elliot Richardson had resigned rather than issue that order to Cox; that the deputy attorney general, William Ruckelshaus, also had refused to do so and had been fired for refusing; that it was a third acting attorney general who had finally issued the order. With trembling voices, television newscasters reported that the President had abolished the office of special prosecutor and that the FBI was standing guard over its files. Never before in our history had a President, setting law at defiance, made our government seem so tawdry and gimcrack. "It's like living in a banana republic," a friend of mine remarked.

Now the question before the country was clear. "Whether ours shall continue to be a government of laws and not of men," the ex-special prosecutor said that evening, "is now for the Congress and ultimately the American people to decide."

Within ten days of the "Saturday night massacre," one million letters and telegrams rained down on Congress, almost every one of them demanding the President's impeachment. But congressional leaders dragged their feet. The House Judiciary Committee would begin an inquiry into *whether* to begin an inquiry into possible grounds for recommending impeachment to the House. With the obvious intent, it seemed to me, of waiting until the impeachment fervor had abated, the Democratic-controlled committee would consider whether to consider making a recommendation about making an accusation.

Republicans hoped to avoid upholding the rule of law by persuading the President to resign. This attempt to supply a lawless remedy for lawless power earned Republicans a memorable rebuke from one of the most venerated members of their party: eighty-one-year-old Sen. George Aiken of Vermont. The demand for Nixon's resignation, he said, "suggests that many prominent Americans, who ought to know better, find the task of holding a President accountable as just too difficult. . . . To ask the President now to resign and thus relieve Congress of its clear congressional duty amounts to a declaration of incompetence on the part of Congress."

The system was manifestly not working. But neither was the President's defense. On national television Nixon bitterly assailed the press for its "outrageous, vicious, distorted" reporting, but the popular outrage convinced him, nonetheless, to surrender the nine tapes to the court. Almost at once the White House tapes began their singular career of encompassing the President's ruin. On October 31 the White House disclosed that two of the taped conversations were missing, including one between the President and his campaign manager, John Mitchell, which had taken place the day after Nixon returned from a Florida vacation and three days after the Watergate break-in. Three weeks later the tapes dealt Nixon a more potent blow. There was an eighteen-and-a-half-minute gap, the White House announced, in a taped conversation between the President and Haldeman, which had also taken place the day after he returned from Florida. The White House suggested first that the President's secretary, Rose Mary Woods, had accidentally erased part of the tape while transcribing it. When the loyal Miss Woods could not demonstrate in court how she could have pressed the "erase" button unwittingly for eighteen straight minutes, the White House attributed the gap to "some sinister force." On January 15, 1974, court-appointed experts provided a more humdrum explanation. The gap had been produced by at least five manual erasures. Someone in the White House had deliberately destroyed evidence that might have proved that President Nixon knew of the Watergate cover-up from the start.

At this point the Judiciary Committee was in its third month of considering whether to consider. But by now there was scarcely an American who did not think the President guilty, and on February 6, 1974, the House voted 410 to 4 to authorize the Judiciary Committee to begin investigating possible grounds for impeaching the President of the United States. It had taken ten consecutive months of the most damning revelations of criminal misconduct, a titanic outburst of public indignation, and an unbroken record of presidential deceit, defiance, and evasion in order to compel Congress to take its first real step. That long record of immobility and feigned indifference boded ill for the future.

The White House knew how to exploit congressional reluctance. One tactic involved a highly technical but momentous question: What constituted an impeachable offense? On February 21 the staff of the Judiciary Committee had issued a report. Led by two distinguished attorneys, John Doar, a fifty-two-year-old Wisconsin Independent, and Albert Jenner, a sixty-seven-year-old Chicago Republican, the staff had taken the broad view of impeachment for which Hamilton and Madison had contended in *The Federalist Papers*. Despite the constitutional phrase "high Crimes and Misdemeanors," the staff report had argued that an impeachable offense did not have to be a crime. "Some of the most grievous offenses against our Constitutional form of government may not entail violations of the criminal law."

The White House launched a powerful counterattack. At a news conference on February 25, the President contended that only proven criminal misconduct supplied grounds for impeachment. On February 28, the White House drove home his point with a tightly argued legal paper: If a President could be impeached for anything other than a crime of "a very serious nature," it would expose the Presidency to "political impeachments."

The argument was plausible. But if Congress accepted it, the Watergate crisis could only end in disaster. Men of great power do not commit crimes. They procure crimes without having to issue incriminating orders. A word to the servile suffices. "Who will free me from this turbulent priest," asked Henry II, and four of his barons bashed in the skull of Thomas à Becket. The ease with which the powerful can arrange "deniability," to use the Watergate catchword, was one reason the criminal standard was so dangerous to liberty. Instead of having to take care that the laws be faithfully executed, a President, under that standard, would only have to take care to insulate himself from the criminal activities of his agents. Moreover, the standard could not reach the most dangerous offenses. There is no crime in the statute books called "attempted tyranny."

Yet the White House campaign to narrow the definition of impeachment met with immediate success. In March one of the members of the House of Representatives said that before voting to impeach Nixon, he would "want to know beyond a reasonable doubt that he was directly involved in the commission of a crime." To impeach the President for the grave abuse of his powers, lawmakers said, would be politically impossible. On the Judiciary Committee itself the senior Republican, Edward Hutchinson of Michigan, disavowed the staff's view of impeachment and adopted the President's. Until the final days of the crisis, the criminal definition of impeachment was to hang over the country's fate like the sword of Damocles.

The criminal standard buttressed the President's larger thesis: In defending himself he was fighting to protect the "Presidency" from sinister forces trying to "weaken" it. On March 12 the President's lawyer, James D. St. Clair, sounded this theme when he declared that he did not represent the President "individually" but rather the "office of the Presidency." There was even a National Citizens Committee for Fairness to the Presidency. It was America's global leadership, Nixon insisted, that made a "strong" Presidency so essential. Regardless of the opinion of some members of the Judiciary Committee, Nixon told a joint session of Congress, he would do nothing that "impairs the ability of the Presidents of the future to make the great decisions that are so essential to this nation and the world."

I used to listen to statements such as these with deep exasperation. Here was a President daring to tell Congress, in effect, that a lawless Presidency was necessary to America's safety, while a congressional attempt to reassert the rule of law undermined the nation's security.

Fortunately for constitutional government, however, Nixon's conception of a strong Presidency included one prerogative whose exercise was in itself an impeachable offense. Throughout the month of March the President insisted that the need for "confidentiality" allowed him to withhold forty-two tapes that the Judiciary Committee had asked of him. Nixon was claiming the right to limit the constitutional power of Congress to inquire into his impeachment. This was more than Republicans on the committee could afford to tolerate.

"Ambition must be made to counteract ambition," Madison had written in *The Federalist*. On April 11 the Judiciary Committee voted 33 to 3 to subpoena the forty-two tapes, the first subpoena ever issued to a

President by a committee of the House. Ambition, at last, was counteracting ambition. This set the stage for one of the most lurid moments in the entire Watergate crisis.

As the deadline for compliance drew near, tension began mounting in the country. Comply or defy? Which would the President do? Open defiance was plainly impeachable. Frank compliance was presumably ruinous. On Monday, April 29, the President went on television to give the American people his answer. Seated in the Oval Office with the American flag behind him, President Nixon calmly announced that he was going to make over to the Judiciary Committee — and the public — "edited transcripts" of the subpoenaed tapes. These transcripts "Will tell it all," said the President; there was nothing more that would need to be known for an impeachment inquiry about his conduct. To sharpen the public impression of presidential candor, the transcripts had been distributed among forty-two thick, loose-leaf binders, which were stacked in two-foot-high piles by the President's desk. As if to warn the public not to trust what the newspapers would say about the transcripts, Nixon accused the media of concocting the Watergate crisis out of "rumor, gossip, innuendo," of creating a "vague, general impression of massive wrongdoing, implicating everybody, gaining credibility by its endless repetition."

The next day's *New York Times* pronounced the President's speech "his most powerful Watergate defense since the scandal broke." By May 1 James Reston, the newspaper's most eminent columnist, thought the President had "probably gained considerable support in the country." For a few days it seemed as though the President had pulled off a coup. Republicans on the Judiciary Committee acted accordingly. On the first of May, 16 of the 17 committee Republicans voted against sending the President a note advising him that self-edited transcripts punctured by hundreds upon hundreds of suspicious "inaudibles" and "unintelligibles" were not in compliance with the committee's subpoena. The President, it was said, had succeeded in making impeachment look "partisan" and consequently discreditable.

Not even bowdlerized transcripts, however, could nullify the destructive power of those tapes. They revealed a White House steeped in more sordid conniving than Nixon's worst enemies had imagined. They showed a President advising his aides on how to "stonewall" a grand jury without committing perjury:"You can say, 'I don't remember.' You can say, 'I can't recall. I can't give any answer to that, that I can recall.'" They showed a President urging his counsel to make a "complete report" about Watergate but to "make it very incomplete." They showed a President eager for vengeance against ordinary election opponents. "I want the most comprehensive notes on all those who tried to do us in. . . . They are asking for it and they are going to get it." It showed a President discussing how "national security grounds" might be invoked to justify the Ellsberg burglary should the secret ever come out. "I think we could get by on that," replies Nixon's counsel.

On May 7 Pennsylvania's Hugh Scott, Senate Republican Minority Leader, pronounced the revelations in the transcript "disgusting, shabby, immoral performances." Joseph Alsop, who had long been friendly toward the President in his column, compared the atmosphere in the Oval Office to the "back room of a second-rate advertising agency in a suburb of hell." A week after Nixon's seeming coup Republicans were once again vainly urging him to resign. On May 9 the House Judiciary Committee staff began presenting to the members its massive accumulation of Watergate material. Since the presentation was made behind closed doors, a suspenseful lull fell over the Watergate battleground.

Over the next two months it was obvious that the Judiciary Committee was growing increasingly impatient with the President, who continued to insist that, even in an impeachment proceeding, the "executive must remain the final arbiter of demands on its confidentiality." When Nixon refused to comply in any way with a second committee subpoena, the members voted 28 to 10 to warn him that "your refusals in and of themselves might constitute a ground for impeachment." The "partisanship" of May 1 had faded by May 30.

Undermining these signs of decisiveness was the continued insistence that only direct presidential involvement in a crime would be regarded as an impeachable offense in the House. Congressmen demanded to see the "smoking gun." They wanted to be shown the "hand in the cookie jar." Alexander Hamilton had called impeachment a "National Inquest." Congress seemed bent on restricting it to the purview of a local courthouse. Nobody spoke of the larger issues. As James Reston noted on May 26, one of the most disturbing aspects of Watergate was the silence of the prominent. Where, Reston asked, were the educators, the business leaders, and the elder statesmen to delineate and define the great constitutional issues at stake? When the White House began denouncing the Judiciary Committee as a "lynch mob," virtually nobody rose to the committee's defense.

On July 7 the Sunday edition of the *New York Times* made doleful reading. "The official investigations seem beset by semitropical torpor," the newspaper reported in its weekly news summary. White House attacks on the committee, said the *Times*, were proving effective in the country. In March, 60 percent of those polled by Gallup wanted the President tried in the Senate for his misdeeds. By June the figure had fallen to 50 percent. The movement for impeachment, said the *Times*, was losing its momentum. Nixon, it seemed, had worn out the public capacity for righteous indignation.

Then, on July 19, John Doar, the Democrats' counsel, did what nobody had done before with the enormous, confusing mass of interconnected misdeeds that we labeled "Watergate" for sheer convenience. At a meeting of the Judiciary Committee he compressed the endlessly ramified scandal into a grave and compelling case for impeaching the thirty-seventh President of the United States. He spoke of the President's "enormous crimes." He warned the committee that it dare not look indifferently upon the "terrible deed of subverting the Constitution." He urged the members to consider with favor five broad articles of impeachment, charges with a grave historic ring, as the *Times* said of them.

In a brief statement, Albert Jenner, the Republicans' counsel, strongly endorsed Doar's recommendations. The Founding Fathers, he reminded committee members, had established a free country and a free Constitution. It was now the committee's momentous duty to determine "whether that country and that Constitution are to be preserved."

How I had yearned for those words during the long, arid months of the "smoking gun" and the "hand in the cookie jar." Members of the committee must have felt the same way, too, for Jenner's words were to leave a profound mark on their final deliberations. That I did not know yet, but what I did know was heartening. The grave maxims of liberty, once invoked, instantly took the measure of meanness and effrontery. When the President's press spokesman, Ron Ziegler, denounced the committee's proceedings as a "kangaroo court," a wave of disgust coursed through Congress. The hour of the Founders had arrived. The final deliberations of the House Judiciary Committee began on the evening of July 24, when Chairman Peter Rodino gaveled the committee to order before some forty-five million television viewers. The committee made a curious spectacle: thirty-eight strangers strung out on a two-tiered dais, a huge piece of furniture as unfamiliar as the faces of its occupants.

Chairman Rodino made the first opening remarks. His public career had been long, unblemished, and thoroughly undistinguished. Now the representative from Newark, New Jersey, linked hands with the Founding Fathers of our government. "For more than two years, there have been serious allegations, by people of good faith and sound intelligence, that the President, Richard M. Nixon, has committed grave and systematic violations of the Constitution." The framers of our Constitution, said Rodino, had provided an exact measure of a President's responsibilities.

It was by the terms of the President's oath of office, prescribed in the Constitution, that the framers intended to hold Presidents "accountable and lawful."

That was to prove the keynote. That evening and over the following days, as each committee member delivered a statement, it became increasingly clear that the broad maxims of constitutional supremacy had taken command of the impeachment inquiry. "We will by this impeachment proceeding be establishing a standard of conduct for the President of the United States which will for all time be a matter of public record," Caldwell Butler, a conservative Virginia Republican, reminded his conservative constituents. "If we fail to impeach . . . we will have left condoned and unpunished an abuse of power totally without justification."

There were still White House loyalists of course, men who kept demanding to see a presidential directive ordering a crime and a documented "tie-in" between Nixon and his henchmen. Set against the great principle of constitutional supremacy, however, this common view was now exposed for what it was: reckless trifling with our ancient liberties. Can the United States permit a President "to escape accountability because he may choose to deal behind closed doors," asked James Mann, a South Carolina conservative. "Can anyone argue," asked George Danielson, a California liberal, "that if a President breaches his oath of office, he should not be removed?" In a voice of unforgettable power and richness, Barbara Jordan, a black legislator from Texas, sounded the grand theme of the committee with particular depth of feeling. Once, she said, the Constitution had excluded people of her race, but that evil had been remedied. "My faith in the Constitution is whole, it is complete, it is total and I am not going to sit here and be an idle spectator to the diminution, the subversion, the destruction of the Constitution."

On July 27 the Judiciary Committee voted 27 to 11 (six Republicans joining all twenty-one Democrats) to impeach Richard Nixon on the grounds that he and his agents had "prevented, obstructed, and impeded the administration of justice" in "violation of his constitutional oath faithfully to execute the office of President of the United States and, to the best of his ability, preserve, protect, and defend the Constitution of the United States, and in violation of his constitutional duty to take care that the laws be faithfully executed."

On July 29 the Judiciary Committee voted 28 to 10 to impeach Richard Nixon for "violating the constitutional rights of citizens, impairing the due and proper administration of justice and the conduct of lawful inquiries, or contravening the laws governing agencies of the executive branch. . . ." Thus, the illegal wiretaps, the sinister White House spies, the attempted use of the IRS to punish political opponents, the abuse of the CIA, and the break-in at Ellsberg's psychiatrist's office — misconduct hitherto deemed too "vague" for impeachment — now became part of a President's impeachable failure to abide by his constitutional oath to carry out his constitutional duty.

Lastly, on July 30 the Judiciary Committee, hoping to protect some future impeachment inquiry from a repetition of Nixon's defiance, voted 21 to 17 to impeach him for refusing to comply with the committee's subpoenas. "This concludes the work of the committee," Rodino announced at eleven o'clock that night. Armed with the wisdom of the Founders and the authority of America's republican principles, the committee had cut through the smoke screens, the lies, and the pettifogging that had muddled the Watergate crisis for so many months. It had subjected an imperious Presidency to the rule of fundamental law. It had demonstrated by resounding majorities that holding a President accountable is neither "liberal" nor "conservative," neither "Democratic" nor "Republican," but something far more basic to the American republic.

For months the forces of evasion had claimed that impeachment would "tear the country apart." But now the country was more united than it had been in years. The impeachment inquiry had sounded the chords of deepest patriotism, and Americans responded, it seemed to me, with quiet pride in their country and themselves. On Capitol Hill, congressional leaders reported that Nixon's impeachment would command three hundred votes at a minimum. The Senate began preparing for the President's trial. Then, as countless wits remarked, a funny thing happened on the way to the forum.

Back on July 24, the day the Judiciary Committee began its televised deliberations, the Supreme Court had ordered the President to surrender sixty-four taped conversations subpoenaed by the Watergate prosecutor. At the time I had regarded the decision chiefly as an auspicious omen for the evening's proceedings. Only Richard Nixon knew that the Court had signed his death warrant. On August 5 the President announced that he was making public three tapes that "may further damage my case." In fact they destroyed what little was left of it. Recorded six days after the Watergate break-in, they showed the President discussing detailed preparations for the cover-up with his chief of staff, Bob Haldeman. They showed the President and his henchman discussing how to use the CIA to block the FBI, which was coming dangerously close to the White House. "You call them in," says the President. "Good deal," says his aide. In short, the three tapes proved that the President had told nothing but lies about Watergate for twenty-six months. Every one of Nixon's ten

Judiciary Committee defenders now announced that he favored Nixon's impeachment.

The President still had one last evasion: on the evening of August 8 he appeared on television to make his last important announcement. "I no longer have a strong enough political base in Congress," said Nixon, doing his best to imply that the resolution of a great constitutional crisis was mere maneuvering for political advantage. "Therefore, I shall resign the Presidency effective at noon tomorrow." He admitted to no wrongdoing. If he had made mistakes of judgment, "they were made in what I believed at the time to be in the best interests of the nation."

On the morning of August 9 the first President ever to resign from office boarded Air Force One and left town. The "system" had worked. But in the watches of the night, who has not asked himself now and then: How would it all have turned out had there been no White House tapes?*

At the time of Richard Nixon's resignation from the Presidency, columnists, politicians, and other sages spoke woefully of the tragedy of Watergate, or the trauma of Watergate, depending on whether their sense of language was Shakespearean or psychiatric. They were, in either case, Washington folk, and apparently not much aware that many of us, out in the country, looked on the thing more as the triumph of Watergate, or even, depending on the length of our standing as Nixon-haters, the Watergate comedy hour — with Groucho Liddy, Harpo Hunt in the red wig, and the President as Zeppo, the straight brother who sings at the end of the show. Martha Mitchell was perfect as Margaret Dumont, and there were several candidates for Chico, Charles Colson for one, though my favorite was Donald Segretti, the busy young California lawyer who signed himself on as an expert in dirty tricks.

If there were gleeful, hard-nosed scapegraces who watched Watergate that way, our laughter had, I confess, a paranoid nervousness much of the time. We could never feel sure that Nixon, Haig, and Kissinger would not engineer America's first military take-over, in preference to its first presidential act of self-destruction. Not until we saw the final helicopter lift off from the White House garden could we really relax and enjoy it all.

I enjoy it less in perspective, and I sympathize more with the leading

*Walter Karp's account ends here. Vance Bourjaily's account begins below.

player. I have come to see Watergate not as a complete tragedy but as the last act of a terribly extended one, which opened in crazy violence with the assassination of John Kennedy.

It was Greek in form, rather than Elizabethan, a democratic rather than a royal tragedy. This was largely because of the participation of a chorus of around two hundred million. Much of the long sequence concerned the fall of the great Kennedy family, whose antagonist Nixon was. But interwoven was the division of a once-united nation, whose people passionately took sides on the conduct of a distant war and on the demands for power at home of their minorities—the blacks, the women, and the young.

Remembered in this way, it ended in Aristotelian catharsis. Richard Nixon was a doomed anti-hero, whose coerced self-sacrifice, with true irony, realized his campaign slogan in bringing us together. Remembered in this way Watergate was what we needed. . . .

Questions for Discussion

1. Should a president ever be able to assert executive privilege on the grounds of national security, and thus not have to turn over evidence in a criminal proceeding? If so, in what circumstances?

2. Was President Gerald Ford right to pardon Richard Nixon? Did the pardon enable the nation to put Watergate behind it and move on to handle other pressing problems?

3. Did Richard Nixon engage in behavior that was decidedly worse than that of other modern presidents, or did he just happen to get caught? Were Nixon's excesses the product of his own psychological flaws, or does the contemporary political system tend to draw people with certain personality traits? How would you compare the impeachment proceedings against Richard Nixon with those against President Bill Clinton?

12 Firewall: The Iran-Contra Conspiracy and Cover-up

LAWRENCE E. WALSH

For many presidents, it is their leadership in foreign policy that brings greatness to their legacies. The president typically has wider latitude in conducting foreign policy, but such activity also has its pitfalls. In this selection, Independent Counsel Lawrence Walsh relates how the Iran-Contra Scandal was one such foreign policy imbroglio: The Reagan administration became its own willing victim by pursuing a confused ethic, believing what wasn't so, and ultimately breaking the law.

ON MONDAY, NOVEMBER 24, 1986, Ronald Reagan left his handsome Oval Office, passed the bright cabinet room, and descended to the situation room in the White House basement. The low-ceilinged, tightly shuttered conference room looked nothing like the bustling war-time military command post its name suggested. The President sat at the end of a long conference table, between Vice President George Bush, Secretary of Defense Caspar Weinberger, Director of Central Intelligence William Casey, and National Security Advisor John Poindexter on his right and Secretary of State George Shultz, Attorney General Edwin Meese, and Chief of Staff Donald Regan on his left. The chairs along the walls, where subordinate staff members usually sat, were empty. A single CIA official had made a report and then left. The taping equipment that sometimes recorded presidential meetings was shut off. The cabinet members took their own notes.

Reagan was within range of impeachment for his secret authorization of the sale of American weapons to Iran in exchange for American hostages, which had violated not only the Arms Export Control Act and the National Security Act but also his own stated policy against dealing with terrorists. Moreover, breaking the cardinal rule of covert operatives, he had begun to believe his own cover: He had persuaded himself that he had not been trading arms for hostages; he had merely tried to establish a friendly relationship with Iranian moderates.

Sitting next to the president, the secretary of state was weighing resignation against the danger of dismissal. Weinberger and Casey, angered by Shultz's unwillingness to support the arms sales publicly, were eager to see him go. As the meeting began, Shultz and Poindexter battled for the president's ear over control of negotiations with Iran. After they wore each other down, Donald Regan turned the discussion to Meese, who, perhaps more than anyone else in the room, felt a personal responsibility for the president's political safety. Regan had that official responsibility, but Meese was the president's most devoted troubleshooter. He had been counselor to the president before becoming attorney general and he had long served under Reagan in California and in political campaigns.

The sequence of events that necessitated this meeting had begun in 1979, with the overthrow of the shah of Iran and the seizure of the U.S. embassy in Tehran by radical Iranians loyal to an aged Islamic leader, the Ayatollah Ruhollah Khomeini. With its embassy's staff held hostage, the United States had broken diplomatic relations and embargoed trade with Iran. After the hostages were released, the United States made some concessions to Iran but continued to embargo arms shipments. In the meantime, Iraq had opened war on Iran. The United States remained neutral and refused to ship arms to either side.

On January 20, 1984, the secretary of state designated Iran a sponsor of international terrorism. Thereafter, in what was called "Operation Staunch," the United States actively urged its allies not to ship arms to Iran.

Beginning in March 1984, members of Hezbollah, a fundamentalist Shiite group sympathetic to the government of the Ayatollah Khomeini, kidnapped seven Americans — including William Buckley, the CIA chief of station — in Beirut, Lebanon. The United States and, in particular, President Reagan adamantly opposed dealing with hostage takers. "America will never make concessions to terrorists — to do so would only invite more terrorism," he stated to the press on June 18, 1985. "Once we head down that path, there would be no end to it." Three weeks later, I heard him say much the same thing in a speech to the annual meeting of the American Bar Association. The members responded with cheers and a standing ovation.

Not all American foreign policy experts favored the isolation of Iran. Poindexter's predecessor as national security advisor, Robert "Bud" McFarlane, had been concerned with a possible Soviet move after the death of the Ayatollah Khomeini. With support from the CIA, McFarlane had analyzed the feasibility of establishing better relations with moderate Iranians and relaxing the arms embargo to reduce the danger of Iran's being proselytized by the Soviet Union. This tampering with the embargo had been vehemently rejected by Shultz and Weinberger. Iran was desperate for weapons to use in its war with Iraq, however, and various Iranians approached U.S. officials with offers to help free the hostages in Lebanon in exchange for arms. In the summer of 1985, an offer from an Iranian arms broker, Manucher Ghorbanifar, found its way to McFarlane through Israeli intermediaries.

Despite the strong views of Shultz and Weinberger, the high-level Israelis persuaded McFarlane to explore with the president the possibility of discussions with the Iranians. The weapons were said to be merely a token of the administration's good faith to establish the credibility of the Iranian negotiators in their own country. If they succeeded in freeing the hostages, Israel would sell the Iranians missiles that Israel had previously obtained from the United States; the Israelis would then buy replacements from the United States. Casey supported McFarlane. Shultz and Weinberger questioned the likelihood of any favorable changes in our relations with Iran, and they vigorously opposed arms sales to Iran by any nation. Nonetheless, after reflection, the president approved the transaction. Israel, through Ghorbanifar and its private intermediaries shipped ninety-six wire-guided antitank (TOW) missiles to Iran on August 30 and another 408 on September 14. One hostage was released.

In mid-November, McFarlane and Poindexter learned from Lieutenant Colonel Oliver North, the National Security Council counterterrorism expert who kept them abreast of the Israeli arms shipments, that a much larger Israeli arms sale was in train. They informed the president, the vice president, Regan, Casey, and Shultz. Israel was to sell as many as five hundred large Hawk antiaircraft missiles to Iran, with replacements to be supplied by the United States. At least four hostages were to be released.

To locate enough Hawks to replenish Israel's arsenal, McFarlane telephoned Weinberger. The defense secretary protested that the shipment would be illegal, but McFarlane told him that the president had decided the matter. Shultz disapproved of the operation but agreed not to stand in the way.

There were logistical problems, however, because Israeli aircraft carrying weapons could not fly directly to Iran. After the privately chartered aircraft carrying the first shipment had lifted off from Israel, officials in the European country where the Hawks were to be transferred to planes of a different nationality for delivery to Iran unexpectedly denied permission for the cargo to land. The Israeli defense minister telephoned McFarlane for help. He turned to Oliver North, who drew in the CIA, arranging for one of the agency's proprietary air fleets to carry the first installment of the shipment to Iran.

The shipment was a disaster on all counts. Only about eighty Hawks had been available, and when the first eighteen were delivered on November 24, the Iranians were outraged to find that the shipment consisted of outdated Israeli castoffs with the Star of David stenciled on them. At the CIA, John McMahon, the acting director (in Casey's absence), was dumbfounded and then furious to learn of the agency's participation. To provide political and legal cover for the agency, McMahon and Casey promptly obtained a retroactive finding from the president approving the CIA's action.

Fearing for the hostages' safety, the president urgently convened a Saturday-morning session of the National Security Planning Group, the high-level core of the National Security Council. The NSC consisted of four statutory members: the president, the vice president, the secretary of state, and the secretary of defense. Additional invited members had traditionally included the head of the CIA and the chairman of the Joint Chiefs of Staff, but President Reagan had invited so many others to NSC meetings over the years that the NSPG was established to deal with the most sensitive and important issues.

When the group met in the president's residential quarters, Weinberger explicitly warned that the U.S. arms embargo imposed against Iran in 1979 and strengthened in 1983 made the sale of any weapons illegal even if it was carried out through the Israelis. Moreover, the Arms Export Control Act provided that the resale of so large a quantity of arms by a foreign recipient had to be authorized by the president with notice to Congress.

Dismissing Weinberger's objections, the president declared that "he could answer charges of illegality but he couldn't answer [the] charge that 'big strong President Reagan passed up a chance to free hostages.' " Jokingly, he remarked that if he went to jail, "visiting hours are Thursday."

Weinberger rejoined that Reagan would not be alone.

The consensus of the meeting had been to stop the arms sales and, for the time being, to limit discussions to the improvement of U.S.-Iranian relations. McFarlane delivered this message to Ghorbanifar and the Israeli representatives, but Ghorbanifar refused to relay it to his principals, arguing that the message would be tantamount to a death warrant for the hostages. Although McFarlane advised Reagan to end the negotiations, other Israeli proposals were pressed on the president.

After two more NSPG meetings in January 1986, the president ordered Poindexter and the CIA to drop the Israelis as middlemen and to negotiate a direct sale of arms from the United States to Iran. Reagan signed a presidential finding, which he kept secret from Congress, authorizing the sale. "I agreed to sell TOWs to Iran," he noted in his diary for January 17.

This new covert action was undertaken by Poindexter and North, with the CIA in a supporting role. The financial negotiations and the arms deliveries were handled by North and retired Air Force major general Richard Secord, who was also working with North to resupply the Contras in Nicaragua. North and Secord dealt with Ghorbanifar and midlevel Iranian officials.

Secord delivered a thousand U.S. TOW missiles to Iran in February. Ghorbanifar had paid Secord in advance. Secord had paid the CIA in advance. The CIA had bought the weapons from the Department of Defense at cost. With Poindexter's approval, North and Secord had marked up the price almost threefold — from $3.7 million to $10 million — and kept the extra proceeds to pay for arms for the Contras and for other purposes unauthorized by Congress. No hostages were freed.

In May, at President Reagan's request, McFarlane led a secret mission with North and others to Tehran to deliver two planeloads of spare parts for Hawk missiles and to recover the hostages. After three and a half frustrating days, McFarlane reported failure. He had delivered one planeload of parts, but when this failed to win the release of any more hostages, he held back the second planeload. On his return, he repeated his previous advice to the president: Quit.

Still Ronald Reagan pressed on. After six more weeks, a second hostage was released, so the president authorized the delivery of the second load of Hawk spare parts. North had marked the prices up by 370 percent, and Ghorbanifar had added a markup of his own. The Iranians discovered the markups, however, and refused to pay. Ghorbanifar, as an intermediary, had borrowed to prepay Secord for the U.S. matériel. Secord had already used part of the payment to buy arms for the Contras. While Ghorbanifar haggled with the Iranians for reimbursement, another Iranian intermediary negotiated the sale of five hundred more TOW missiles. Hezbollah then played a cynical hand: As one group of kidnappers was about to release a third hostage, another group kidnapped two more.

On November 3, the plot unraveled. A Lebanese periodical, *Al Shiraa*, published a story revealing that the United States had sold arms to Iran. The article also detailed McFarlane's failed mission to Tehran, portraying McFarlane as a supplicant and North as a naive amateur carrying a Bible and a chocolate cake. Picked up by the news media in the United States and abroad, and confirmed by the speaker of the Iranian parliament, Ali Akbar Rafsanjani, the story could not be ignored.

From the beginning, the White House had looked for ways to suppress the truth. The story had "no foundation," President Reagan assured reporters on November 6, and publicity about it was "making it more difficult for us in our effort to get the other hostages free." In his diary the next day, he sketched his approach: "We can't and won't answer [questions] because [to do so] would endanger those we are trying to help."

Vice President George Bush, who had just begun keeping a diary, also understood the need for secrecy. "I'm one of the few people that know fully the details," he wrote on November 5, "and there is a lot of flack and misinformation out there. It is not a subject we can talk about."

Poindexter and Casey argued forcefully against any disclosure. Both encouraged North to continue his secret negotiations with emissaries from Tehran.

Meanwhile, journalists energetically pursued the story. Rafsanjani supplied additional details of McFarlane's visit. Don Regan fingered McFarlane, in anonymous comments to magazine reporters, as the central culprit in humiliating the nation.

McFarlane had at first brushed off the story as "fanciful." On hearing that Regan was blaming him, however, he exploded in an angry computer message to Poindexter, threatening to sue Regan for singling him out for a policy that had received collective, though not unanimous, top-level endorsement from the start. Poindexter reported back that Regan "would keep his mouth shut."

On November 8, McFarlane sent a message to North concerning the records of the National Security Agency, an intelligence agency that had been monitoring the arms deals: "I hope to daylights that someone has been purging the NSA's files on this episode." North was already shredding and altering documents from his office and from the permanent files of the National Security Council.

Secretary of Defense Weinberger complained to Poindexter that the secretary of state had "suggested 'telling all' on attempts to deal with Iran to get their help." According to his notes, Weinberger had "strongly objected. I said we should simply say nothing — John [Poindexter] agrees."

This division deepened in a meeting of the National Security Planning Group on November 10. In a ninety-minute session at the White House, Reagan, Bush, Regan, Poindexter, Casey, Shultz, Weinberger, and Meese discussed the administration's dealings with Iran but could not reach a consensus about what to acknowledge publicly. Only Shultz wanted to concede the failure and try to defend it.

Donald Regan preferred a response more forthcoming than "no comment," as he noted on November 10: "We must get a statement out now, we are being attacked, and we are being hurt."

The president put the issue more colorfully. "We must say something but not much. I'm being held out to dry."

Admiral Poindexter, still hoping the stonewall would hold, warned that any acknowledgment of the arms deals would "end our Iranian contacts." If there had to be a statement, he thought, it should "say less about what we are doing and more about what we are not doing."

Poindexter drew the line at exposing the 1985 Israeli transactions, which the president had approved without notifying Congress. In briefing the NSPG, Poindexter falsely claimed that Israel had sold U.S. arms in 1985 without our permission; that we had only accidentally discovered the arms en route to Iran in a European warehouse; and that the presidentially approved sales had begun only after January 1986, when the president had signed a finding formally authorizing direct sales to Iran. Poindexter made no mention of the Hawks delivered in November 1985.

Shultz pressed Reagan for a commitment that no more arms would go to Iran, but his proposal drew no support. After the meeting, a White House press release stressed concern for the safety of the hostages and pledged that "no U.S. laws have been or will be violated and . . . [that] our policy of not making concessions to terrorists remains intact." President Reagan "asked his advisors to ensure that their departments refrain from making comments or speculating about these matters." Before being released, the statement had to be revised because Shultz rejected a proposed reference to the "unanimous support for the president's policies." At his insistence, the final version recited only "unanimous support for the president."

To his aides, Shultz fumed that the press release showed that the president's advisors were "trying to get me to lie." Whatever they were "trying to pull on me" he added, the maneuver was "taking the president down the drain." The way to halt that slide, he believed, was to make a clean breast of the errors, restore the authority to deal with Iran to his department, and end the freelance operations of the National Security Council's staff.

While presidential aides worried about impeachment, Ronald Reagan considered the public reaction excessive. "This whole irresponsible press bilge about hostages and Iran has gotten totally out of hand," he noted in his diary for November 12. "The media looks like it's trying to create another Watergate. . . . I want to go public personally and tell the people the truth." In an address to the nation broadcast from the Oval Office the next day, the president declared that the dealings with Iran had been aimed primarily at restoring normal relations and only secondarily at freeing Americans held captive in the Middle East. True, Iran had acquired some defensive U.S. weaponry, but the charge that America had been "trafficking with terrorists," he said, was "utterly false."

His audience did not believe him. Polls by the news media and the White House found that for every American who accepted the president's version of events, six others doubted it and him. Ronald Reagan seemed to be deceiving himself. He *had* traded arms for hostages. He had pushed eager aides to keep bargaining when more seasoned officers had advised against it. In his own mind, he had arranged the facts into the context of McFarlane's original proposal of an "Iran initiative" — a secretive effort to open lines of communication and support to factions in Tehran that might someday replace the Ayatollah Khomeini's radical regime with pro-Western policies, and that might, as a gesture of goodwill, persuade their Lebanese followers to release the hostages. In fact, the dialogue had never gone beyond bartering missiles for prisoners. The hidden trade and the diversion of part of the proceeds to the Contras had violated American policy and law.

Two days later, in the situation room, the president and his top advisors fed congressional leaders the false account that had been developed for public consumption. Ronald Reagan described the activity as "principally a covert intelligence operation" that had involved "no negotiations with terrorists" and had been designed "to enhance [America's] position in the Middle East."

Poindexter began his report with the direct sales to Iran authorized by the president's January 1986 finding. Senate Majority Leader Robert Byrd asked when the first contact with Iran had occurred and Poindexter admitted that the process had begun in 1985, but he claimed that "no transfer of material" had taken place until after the presidential finding had been signed

The journalists were more aggressive than the congressional leaders had been. The day after misleading Senator Byrd, Poindexter had to acknowledge to a reporter that a "small amount of stuff" had gone to Iran in connection with the first release of a hostage, the Reverend Benjamin Weir.

McFarlane feared that by lack of candor, the administration might find itself caught up in a scandal on the order of Watergate. In the earlier debacle, he warned Poindexter, "well-meaning people who were in on the early planning of the communications strategy didn't intend to lie but ultimately came around to it." The Reagan White House had to choose, he urged, between ducking and accepting the blame. If the policy was to be defended "on its merits," the manner "must not be confrontational but open and candid."

Calls for congressional inquiries multiplied. After President Reagan's televised speech of November 13, the pressure for a public accounting heightened. The House and Senate intelligence committees scheduled hearings and asked Casey, Shultz, and Poindexter to testify.

Within the administration, concern centered on what to say about the illegal November 1985 Hawk shipment, which exposed the president to the most danger. Both the CIA and Oliver North compiled chronological accounts, which conflicted with each other and with the truth. The narrowly self-protective CIA version said that no one in the agency had known at the time that its proprietary aircraft had carried Hawk missiles rather than oil-drilling equipment. North broadened the claim to say that "no one in the government" had been aware of the cargo's true nature.

Richard Secord, who had arranged with the CIA proprietary for the delivery of the Hawks, was dismayed to read that the president had been upset and that those involved in the transport had thought they were carrying oil-drilling equipment. "The new, phony version would stand," Secord realized. Having believed that his activities had been authorized by the president, he told North, "I guess I get the picture, now. I'll get out of your hair. I'm not going to be a part of this anymore."

Appearing on a Sunday-morning television news show, George Shultz stated that he opposed any further arms transactions with Iran. Asked whether he, as secretary of state, spoke for the whole administration on this policy, Shultz candidly answered that he did not.

Ignoring a direct warning from Shultz that he was being deceived, the president repeated at a news conference on November 19 that he had not traded arms for hostages. He went on to deny that the Israeli shipments had occurred. The White House press office hastily issued a clarifying statement conceding that a "third country" had taken part in "our secret project."

On the evening of November 20, George Shultz and Don Regan visited the president in the family quarters in the White House. For forty-five minutes, Shultz tried without success to get the president to face the truth. Reagan insisted that because he had never *intended* to bargain arms for hostages, he had never done so. Shultz reminded him that McFarlane had told them both about the planned Israeli Hawk shipment during the

November 1985 summit conference with Soviet leader Mikhail Gorbachev in Geneva.

"Oh, I knew about that," replied Reagan, "but that wasn't arms for hostages."

Shultz later told an aide, "I didn't shake him one bit. . . . He refuses to see that we have a problem. So I never got to what should be done."

Casey's prepared testimony to the House intelligence committee the next day simply omitted the Hawks, but in answering questions, he fell back on the canard about the oil equipment. Having denied knowledge that weapons were carried, he could not then reveal that at his request the president had signed a retroactive finding approving the CIA's carrying them.

Just before noon on Friday, November 21, Poindexter, Regan, and Meese met with the president in the Oval Office. Reagan agreed that someone should develop a coherent position for the administration. The assignment went to Meese.

When North and Poindexter learned about the attorney general's mission, they stepped up their efforts to purge their files. North and his secretary, Fawn Hall, shredded a pile of documents, including North's telephone records and copies of his memoranda to McFarlane and Poindexter. They also altered documents taken from the permanent files of the National Security Council. As North and the NSC staff counsel watched, Poindexter calmly tore up the original presidential finding that Ronald Reagan had signed on December 5, 1985, retroactively authorizing the CIA to assist the shipment of the Hawk weapons and specifying that the shipment's purpose was to obtain the release of Americans held hostage in the Middle East.

Over the weekend, the attorney general questioned cabinet officers. He exchanged many telephone calls with Casey and Regan but, departing from his usual practice, took no notes. Meese later claimed that he could not remember what was said. Casey and Regan suffered memory lapses, as well. In an early-Saturday-morning meeting in Shultz's office, Shultz told Meese that the president had admitted knowing about the Hawk shipment. Meese bridled, warning Shultz that if what he said was true and if the president had failed to notify Congress, the law might have been violated. Meese asked whether Shultz knew of any other writings except the notes he had himself dictated. Shultz knew of none.

The attorney general then left to meet with McFarlane, who said that he had told President Reagan about the planned Hawk shipment but that he had nothing in writing. Meese next telephoned Weinberger and concluded that he had little information about the transaction. In reality, Weinberger had preserved notes of his conversations with McFarlane, warning him in advance that the Hawk transaction would be illegal whether carried out through Israel or not.

While Meese talked to the cabinet officers, his assistants found in North's office a draft copy of an April 1986 memorandum in which North explained for Poindexter the diversion of $12 million from the proceeds of the Iran arms sales to rearm the Nicaraguan insurgents known as the Contras. Not only had President Reagan flouted the National Security Act and the Arms Export Control law, but North's illegal use of the proceeds to finance the Contras had usurped Congress's constitutional authority over government appropriations. Because the proceeds should have gone to the U.S. Treasury, the diversion had amounted to theft. The next day, Meese and his assistants questioned North for four hours in what Meese later testified was "a chat among colleagues." North assured Meese that the memorandum had not gone to the president.

Shultz spent that Sunday considering resignation, and others were eager to hurry his departure. Before the weekend was out, William Casey had written to President Reagan to attack "the public pouting of George Shultz" and to recommend that he be replaced by Senator Paul Laxalt of Nevada or by Jeane Kirkpatrick, the U.S. ambassador to the United Nations.

Tension filled the situation room on November 24, as President Reagan pounded the table and insisted that he had not traded arms for hostages, that the sale of missiles was meant to restore normal relations with Iran, that the hostage release was only incidental to it. His undeniable prior knowledge of the Hawk shipment — which had been expressly intended to free the hostages — frustrated any honest effort to develop a coherent position that would exculpate him.

Finally, Reagan turned to Meese for the answer to the critical question: Had the president approved the November 1985 Hawk shipment? Everyone in the room already knew the true answer. Regan had heard the president admit knowledge of the shipment to Shultz on Thursday. Shultz had confirmed this to Meese on Saturday. What was needed now was a political answer.

Before Meese could speak, Poindexter said that McFarlane had handled the Israeli-Iran sales all alone, with no documentation. Meese then fabricated the president's defense. He told the group that although McFarlane had informed Shultz of the planned shipment, McFarlane had not informed the president. Meese warned the group that the shipment might have been a violation of law because the arms had been shipped without notice to Congress. Meese suggested that even after the Hawk shipment, the president had been told only that the hostages would be out in short order.

Regan, who had heard McFarlane inform the president and who had heard the president admit to Shultz that he knew of the shipment of Hawk missiles, said nothing. Shultz and Weinberger, who had protested the shipment before it took place, said nothing. Bush, who had been told of the shipment in advance by McFarlane, said nothing. Casey, who had also known about the shipment ahead of time and had later requested that the president sign the retroactive finding to authorize the CIA-facilitated delivery, said nothing. Poindexter, who had torn up the finding, said nothing. Meese asked whether anyone knew anything else that hadn't been revealed. No one spoke.

Shultz left the meeting early. As always, he immediately dictated notes of the meeting to his executive assistant, Charles Hill. Poindexter's claim that McFarlane had run the operation by himself and that no one had known what he did, Shultz told Hill, was inconsistent with what Shultz knew. They were, he said, "rearranging the record." The president was "now saying he didn't know anything about [McFarlane's] November 1985 activities." The White House was employing, through Meese, a "carefully thought out strategy" to insulate the president and "blame it on Bud" McFarlane.

During the meeting, Meese and Regan had not mentioned the discovery of North's candid outline of the diversion of the arms sales proceeds to the Contras. The simple message they wished to convey to their colleagues was that the president needed to be insulated from the November 1985 Hawk shipment. After the meeting, Meese and Regan followed the president to the Oval Office and told him about the diversion of funds. Reagan seemed genuinely surprised—"as though he had been hit in the stomach," in Regan's words.

Regan, Meese, and Casey then embarked on a desperate gambit, which Regan laid out that day in a memorandum entitled "Plan of Action." "Tough as it seems," he wrote, "blame must be put at NSC's door—rogue operation, going on without president's knowledge or sanction." The goal would be to "try to make the best of a sensational story."

The authors of the plan concluded that it would not be enough to fire North. They needed more than a scapegoat; they needed a firewall. Poindexter had to go. The next day, he resigned at a meeting in which Reagan and Bush expressed their regrets. North, who would be summarily returned to the Marine Corps, received no advance warning of his dismissal; he learned about it on a live television broadcast from the White House.

At noon on November 25, the president and the attorney general went before the White House press corps. The president said he had not been "fully informed on the nature of one of the activities undertaken," which raised "serious questions of propriety." He announced the departures of Poindexter and North, then hurriedly left the podium without taking questions. The job of explaining was left to Meese.

The attorney general had already told his tale that morning, once to cabinet officers and then to congressional leaders, in meetings at the White House. In each case, he omitted reference to the Hawk shipment. He said that the Israelis had handled the arms sales, overcharging the Iranians and depositing the excess funds in Calero's Swiss bank accounts. He said North knew this and Poindexter suspected it. He repeated the falsehood that the president had not learned of the November 1985 Hawk shipment until months afterward.

Shortly before the press conference, an agitated Secord got through to Poindexter on the telephone and asked about rumors that he was resigning. Poindexter confirmed them.

"Stay at your post, admiral," the feisty Secord entreated. "Force the president to step up to the plate and take responsibility for his actions. . . ."

Poindexter replied that time had run out. The attorney general, he said, was about to hold a press conference. The game was over.

Secord felt as if smoke were coming out of his ears. "I would like to talk to the president," he told Poindexter.

"It's too late," said Poindexter. "They're building a wall around him."

Questions for Discussion

1. What do you make of President Reagan's leadership style as evident in the Iran Contra scandal? Should he have been more firmly in touch with the activities of his subordinates, or was his penchant for delegation appropriate? Do you think the President really believed his own rhetoric that his administration was not trading arms for hostages, and that some events transpired without his general knowledge?

2.   Did the members of Reagan's administration (McFarlane, Poindexter, North, Shultz, and others) behave appropriately? What course of action do you think they should have taken when the arms-for-hostages scheme was proposed? Of all the players involved in these events, whose behavior strikes you as least ethical? Whose behavior strikes you as being closest to defensible?

3.   Which was more serious, Watergate or Iran Contra? Nixon resigned before certain impeachment and conviction, whereas Reagan was not even impeached. What were the reasons for the different outcomes? Should Reagan have been impeached and/or convicted? How do Watergate and Iran Contra compare to President Clinton's scandal involving Monica Lewinsky, his faulty grand jury testimony, and subsequent impeachment?

COPYRIGHT
ACKNOWLEDGMENTS